Aleutian Headache

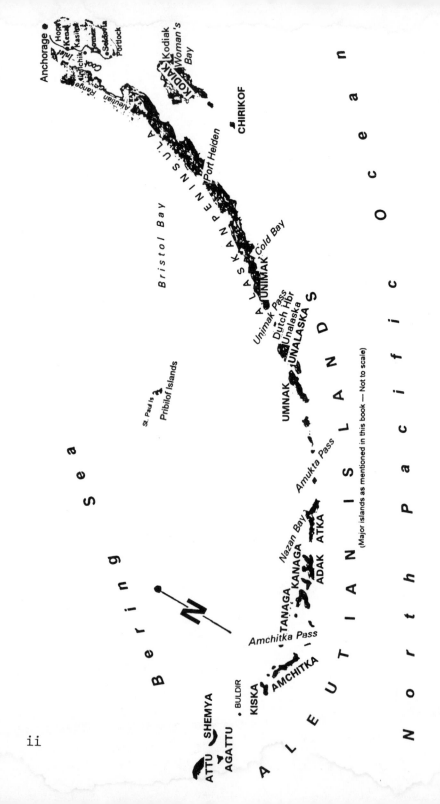

Anchorage
Hope
Kenai
Kasilof
Seldovia
Portlock
Chugchik
Cook Inlet
Aleutian Range
KODIAK
Kodiak
Woman's Bay
CHIRIKOF
ALASKA PENINSULA
Port Heiden
Bristol Bay
Cold Bay
UNIMAK
Unimak Pass
Dutch Hbr
Unalaska
UNALASKA
St. Paul Is.
Pribilof Islands
UMNAK
Amukta Pass
ALEUTIAN ISLANDS
(Major islands as mentioned in this book — Not to scale)
Nazan Bay
ATKA
TANAGA
KANAGA
ADAK
Amchitka Pass
AMCHITKA
KISKA
BULDIR
SHEMYA
ATTU
AGATTU
ALEUTIAN
Bering Sea
N
North Pacific Ocean

ii

Aleutian Headache

Deadly World War II Battles
On American Soil

(Documentry)

Bert Webber

Please address all inquiries to the publisher:

WEBB RESEARCH GROUP
P. O. Box 314
Medford, Oregon 97501 U.S.A.

Some of the text and some of the photographs appeared in the author's books:
Silent Siege (1983), *Silent Siege II* (1988), *Silent Siege III* (1992).

The Cover Pictures: (TOP) PBY patrol bomber;
(CENTER) Quonset hut on Kiska,
(LOWER) Attu; Japanese Special Naval Landing Force, Kiska.

—Errata—

Page 67. Delete last paragraph (above the footnote) as it also appears on page 68 starting with the second line.

Page 79. Delete lines 11-16. In line 18, add word "been" to make read "He had been successful...."

The publisher regrets this inconvenience

Library of Congress Cataloging in Publications Data:

Webber, Bert.
    Aleutian headache : deadly World War II battles on American soil
(documentary) / Bert Webber
    Includes bibliographical references (p.) and index.
    ISBN 0-936738-69-3 (pbk.)
    1. World War, 1939-1945 – Campaigns – Alaska – Aleutian Islands.
  2. Aleutian Islands (Alaska) – History, Military. I. Title.
    D769.7.A4W43 1993   93-418
950.54'28 – dc20   CIP

Contents

It is with pride that the author dedicates this book to:

Admiral James S. Russell, U.S.N. (Retired)
Commanding Officer VP-42
PBY Catalina Patrol Squadron
Aleutian Islands 1941-1942

Introduction

The author's first interest in Alaska was born about a year before the start of World War II for when visiting the girl friend in Seattle, I found that her parents knew people with exciting stories about Alaska who went back and forth regularly. And there were more tales from their friend who was a full-time sea captain on an Alaska Steamship Company vessel. Then it turned out the girl's grandfather, the late Will E. Hudson, was the first newsreel cameraman in the Pacific Northwest and Alaska.

Among Hudson's yarns was one of his having been beset in the ice north of Alaska in 1913 while on cinematographic assignment. Then there was the story he covered for Pathe Newsreel on the trans-Arctic flight of the dirigible *Norge*. His association with aircraft pioneer Carl Ben Eielsen was worth another evening. I kept coming around because of my interest in the girl (we married toward the end of the war) and the obvious adventure and excitement that I was generating just from listening to these people. I was receiving a first-hand overview of what Alaska was about from a very exciting standpoint: These people had been there and were photographing it. It would soon be my turn.

My own small corner of Alaska was twofold. 1) Seward. I was not there long. As a low-ranking enlisted man in the Signal Corps, I was ordered to go ashore carrying the suitcases of an officer. I did so and followed the officer to a bench in the dock's warehouse where he said to but his stuff. Then I went back to the ship, the M.S. *Clevedon*. So much for Seward. 2) This was a longer visit – 22 months – and it was at Kodiak. This all-expense paid trip, sponsored by the U. S. Army, started in mid-July 1941. This venture in Alaska continued until mid-May 1943.

The war got its start for me as it did for everyone on Sunday morning December 7, 1941. I was in town for the services at the Kodiak Community Baptist Church then an afternoon of leisure. But the plan was interrupted in the midst of the sermon of the

Old Woman Mountain and Woman's Bay (foreground) with Kodiak Naval Air Station. Above left end of runway is Fort Greely Army cantonment as it appeared in 1973. In background is St. Paul Harbor and village of Kodiak. This is the harbor the Japanese spy pilot saw during flyover in spring 1942. See photo on page 180.

Rev. Gregory Sears Morony by an announcement that the U. S. was suddenly on a war basis with Japan and we G.I.'s had to abandon the day's plans and go back to the cantonment.

But earlier that morning, the local weekly paper, the *Kodiak Mirror* had printed a 1-sheet **EXTRA** that was being distributed around the village telling what little was known to that time – the Japanese had attacked Pearl Harbor. The local camera store, Helsel's Photo, had made copy negatives of the front page of the paper and was already selling prints on post card blanks to the soldiers who were in town for 5¢ each. Helsel said he expected the army boys would be restricted to the cantonment now that war was started and he'd lose their business. After I begged a little, Helsel shared a spare 4 x 5 inch film of the newspaper front page and agreed to my making and selling prints of it at the post. If I,

EXTRA!!

Kodiak Mirror

THE SEAL OF THE TERRITORY OF ALASKA

"News of America's Last Frontier"

VOL. 1   KODIAK ALASKA, DECEMBER 7 1941   NO. 9

U. S. Declares War

Pearl Harbor Bombed

Official information has been received by General Corlett commander Fort Greely that Pearl Harbor was bombed Sunday morning. No mention was made in the wire of Marilla.

No word has been received from the Associated Press on the bombing. The Alaska Communications system reported wires were being held up at Anchorage by poor reception.

General Corlett met with the business men of town at the city hall Sunday morning and plans were formulated for steps necessary in case of air raids here. A second meeting was called in the afternoon at 3 o'clock.

Via Radio — A direct hit at Pearl Harbor was said to have killed 350 men. Last reports say Guam was bombed also.

Boy Scouts and taxis are cooperating in distributing this extra edition. Lt. Craft announced the blackout at the theatre

Blackout Regulations

Regulations concerning evacuation of women and children, and preparations for fire protection, and further notices will be issued later.

MEETING

Another public meeting will be held Tuesday night at 8:00 at the city hall.

Blackout Tonight

called for 8:00 tonight (Sunday) and will last 15 minutes. All lights must be extinguished, including cars. Power will be shut off at power house. Names will be taken of anyone not complying.

BLACKOUT SIGNAL
One long blast fire siren.

ALL CLEAR SIGNAL
Short blast fire siren.

Local Situation Tense

Military authorities say bombing of the town of Kodiak is a remote possibility, but preparations must be made for the eventuality. The two main concerns are danger from fire and the fact that the lights of the town might locate the naval air station for the enemy.

Tonight's blackout will demonstrate what steps must be taken.

Late Bulletins

Japan is reported to have occupied Wake Island. U. S. possession, and to have taken over the American settlement in Shanghai. It is also reported Japan has taken the American gunboat Wake.

All military and naval forces on the island are on a war footing.

3:45 Radio bulletin states U. S. has made formal declaration of war, and that South American countries have followed suit.

As we go to press no further confirmation was had on first reports that U.S had declared war. Congress has been called to meet tomorrow, and it is said President Roosevelt would ask for a declaration

Defense workers at the naval air station will start on a 10-hour day tomorrow.

Censorship has been placed on all communications between the U. S and its possessions. No A. P. bulletins have come through.

Flash—At 4:25 a London dispatch via NBC said a state of war exists between the Netherlands and Japan.

Flash (AP) — London - The British Sunday formally went to war against Finland Hungary, Rumania today because they are fighting Germany's side against Russia.

NOTICE

Right of way must be given army trucks, equipment and men. Any violation will bring full prosecution.

Signed, Charles Cook
Chief of Police

Village of Kodiak in 1940. Mud-flats show tide is out. School is large building near left upper corner

Fort Greely (top) spring 1942. Area
was cleared in 1970's.

Salmon run on
Buskin River at Fort
Greely. Notice 2 x 12
plank bridge.

10

Final inspection at Camp Clatsop, Oregon before embarking for Kodiak and Dutch Harbor, July 1941.Allan Feitelberg with pair of cross-fox furs in front of Kodiak Bear hide. "Welcome to the Bank of Kodiak" stuffed Kodiak Bear from bank's lobby moved into sunlight for portrait.

as the Signal Corps Unit Photographer, kept buying my photo chemicals and paper from him, he said he'd be satisfied.

I made pictures in my skid-shack darkroom (it was called "Bert's Photo Shack") and sold prints at the fort, mostly to the Post Exchange. This contact with the town photo shop proved valuable when the censorship on the mail started and all parcels were subject to sometimes long delays while they were being "checked for content."

As it turned out, between the deal with Helsel and my rented box at the Kodiak post office, I never had any delays in getting photo supplies or equipment. Of course the army had a fit about the personal post office box when word of it leaked. But there were no regulations prohibiting the renting of post office boxes.

*   *   *

While a number of books have appeared in the past about the World War II years in Alaska and the influence of the military on this great area, most have portrayed the role of the Army, the Air Force, the Navy in an overall picture – but some writers have prepared just "unit histories" – our book presents an early history of the American military buildup as at affected the Aleutians in exciting, historically accurate text. This is coupled with many historical and some contemporary photographs and maps.

In addition, while this is an account of majestic and deadly airplanes, and great steel ships of war on both sides of the issue, and the generals and admirals and some others who directed the operations,, we have been able to locate details of some of the "other side" of the action. We are able to present a a section about handling the mail. The arrival of mail, never often enough and never enough of it, was a major operation of itself.

Many readers of popular histories, and those who depend on television specials for their information, will see in this book there is far more to running a war than what the TV show producers present. One will read here not just about the shooting war, bomb droppings and heavy shelling by big ships, but also about the necessity of good "communications." With the bombing of Dutch Harbor, General Buckner saw clearly laid before him that a far greater effort had to be made with communications. This included not just the dots-and-dashes of code, stringing wires and setting up radios, but a number of other things including getting the Army and the Navy on the same wave lengths.

We will mention that there was a small detachment of Japanese-Americans at Attu who served as translators of enemy messages picked out of the air. Most folks don't know about that but these men were there as part of Buckner's overall communications team.

My unit's experiences at Kodiak varied from no duty whatsoever for weeks after we arrived in "peace time," summer of 1941, to the grueling 12+ hour days 7-days a week right after the war started. We were what ultimately became a detachment of the 14th Signal Service Company and were primarily telephone men.

There were a couple of pole climbers but there were no poles to climb. There was a cable splicer and of course no cables. There were equipment installers and telephone repairmen and switchboard operators and brass-pounding telegraph operators and a couple of crypo men but the only "duty" was staying out of sight and going fishing in the Buskin River.

Lt. Eugene E. Kent, Signal Officer, tries his luck in a creek along the east border of Fort Greely during summer 1941. There was no shortage of fish. The creek was fed by Lake Louise and emptied into the Buskin River.

In the fall of 1941, the unit received a field telephone switch-board – a "BD-40" First World War suitcase affair – that was intended for short time use during maneuvers. It was perched on a pair of saw horses in a closet in the fire station. The "installers" ran lengths of W-110B field wire (3 strands copper - 3 strands steel) to various locations. The wire was strung tree to tree and held in place with wooden knobs through which a 10-penny nail was driven through a center hole. The system worked and that was the object. But when the high-officers needed to have a conference call, the buck private telephone operator had to be ordered away from the board so he couldn't listen. And of course these calls shut down the board for all other uses until the conference was completed. But then suddenly, the system quit.

It was just a few days after the helter-skelter activity that followed the declaration of war when our area was deluged by a blizzard. The immediate result was that every one of those nail-it-knob telephone lines went down. To complicate the situation, due to the chronic shortage of wire, the downed wires had to be salvaged from under tons of snow. Just when this was getting underway, the 151st Engineers outfit was ordered to clear the road with bulldozer-D-8 cats. What wire was in the snow got chewed up and that was the end of that!

That winter the troops at what was by then named Fort Greely, were experiencing what they called "severe" weather. But that storm was nothing compared to what the fellows were experiencing in the Aleutians. We'll have more about the weather as well as pictures of it.

In time, a Western Electric civilian installer arrived with a load of equipment and replaced the field outfit. He set up a single-position (1 telephone operator) 1938-model common-battery tele-phone system. It was excellent in its limited sort of way but was replaced with a 4-position board a year later.

The Army at Fort Greely and the Navy at the Naval Air Station just a couple miles down the unpaved road, did not seem to venture much beyond the traditional role of each especially in peace time. The Navy at Kodiak's Woman's Bay was a state-of-the art concrete and steel operation. The army had wooden 2-story barracks of single-wall non-insulated construction. And there was

14

Dial system Navy
telephone exchange, (left)
Kodiak NAS. "New" Army
switchboard (above) just
installed by Tim Desmond,
contractor (left). Men are
identified in Notes

much else that one might compare. Let's just glimpse at the
telephone systems.

The Navy Telephone Exchange was in a weather-proof steam
heated building. It contained a Strowger Automatic Electric
Company step-by-step rotary dial telephone system. The army
had that antique field-wire suitcase switchboard with a hand
crank to ring the phones. (As we have seen, this was eventually
replaced.) When it was realized the two headquarters could not
talk together because the equipment did not match, the Navy ran a
line, with a dial telephone on the end of it, into the Army Wire
Chief's office where he also kept his bunk. In event of an
emergency, the Navy would dial the Army Signal Corps' Wire
Chief and have to tell the Sergeant the message. The Sergeant
would relay, by voice, into an Army phone that was then plugged
into a post headquarters telephone, what the Navy told him – so

15

went the plan. It took awhile to work out a better method due to equipment limitations on the Army end.

Automatic telephone systems have a switchboard for assorted special services but probably 99 percent of the calls do not go an operator who is attending the board. (In that army system, 100 percent of the calls went through operators.) When the war started, the Navy found itself standing short when it didn't have operators to man their switchboard around the clock so pleaded with the Army for help. Army headquarters said OK – then directed the Signal Officer to cooperate. Only one signalman had any state-side training on automatic dial equipment – yours truly. It was good duty because working at the Navy gave access to the Navy Ship's Store as well as the Navy Commissary. This meant extra food of a quality the Army did not possess.

When war started, the anti-aircraft artillery units moved away from the comfortable barracks life into their field positions. One of the gun positions was on top of the hill into which the Signal Corps photo lab was snuggled. During practice firing at small balloons, the empty shell casings rained down on the corrugated iron roof of the skid-shack darkroom with an exciting but ominous clatter. The rattle of practice firing was as close to the shooting war the men at Kodiak experienced.

*   *   *

Admiral James S. Russell's hands-on experiences in the outer, islands of the Aleutians at a critical time is excitement being relived every time we talk or trade letters. He tells of many of his breath-taking encounters recalling the details today at the experienced age of 90. We have been collaborating about this off-an-on for about ten years. Jim Russell is a prime authority for the actions during the early days of the war in North America's only active theater of war, the Aleutians. We were overjoyed when Admiral Russell accepted the invitation to allow us to dedicate this book to him. I thank him for his expertise and friendliness. A biographical sketch of the Admiral appears in the Appendix.

A word of special thanks goes to Laura Gamino who responded to one of many requests for help with this project in 1984. She heard a late-night radio talkshow where I was guest with "Chicago Eddy," (Ed Schwartz) then on WGN Chicago. (These radio shows have occurred every year on or around every December 7th – Pearl Harbor Day for the last twenty years. The program moved to WLUP for the 1992 annual broadcast.) I was discussing the Japanese attacks on North America in World War II and mentioned that my then new book, *Silent Siege,* had a chapter called "Aleutian Headache." I said I sought to expand this into a book by itself using that chapter heading as its title. The present book is the result of that objective. For some background on this project, she graciously offered her keepsake copy of the unique little book *My Way Was North* by Frank Dufresne. There are first-hand observations in this book about a Japanese "watch-service" (spying!) in the Aleutians in the summer of 1931.

Evan V. Klett, U. S. Fish and Wildlife Service, Adak, was of special assistance with data for this book about the Western Aleutians today. He also provided follow-up information about a unique and elusive subject, the "Adak National Forest" and we thank him warmly.

Clare H. Hanawalt, West Linn, Oregon willingly loaned his picture albums made while he was in Alaska Communications System (1st Signal Service Co. Det.) at Kiska for 17 months. He told us in January 1993 that many of his photos were made with a No. 116 size Kodak box camera. He allowed us to select those that seemed appropriate for this book. His contributions have provided a personal side to this book and we thank him for his interest and help.

Bill Macbeth, also of West Linn, spent Army time at Shemya and at Attu and has provided great assistance as well as the loan of maps and numbers of photographs of his 2½ years at "the outer end." He carried a Leica 35mm camera and used it often. We appreciate his interest and willingness to share his keepsakes and thank him for being willing to help. (See Notes.)

Wayne Gentry, Olympia, Wash., was in the Engineers at Attu (APO 726). We ran on to him during our search into Army Post Offices and found a few of his letters addressed to a "Dear Lucious." He loaned his snapshots of Attu then after some digging the author located "Dear Lucious"-Lou, one Louise Boise of Roseburg, Oregon. She was amazed we could locate each of them fifty years later. (They did not marry each other.) We very much appreciate the interest and help from these two friendly people.

As this book includes material about former Japanese who bombed Dutch Harbor and some who dodged American bombs on Kiska, we appreciate the kind help of translators Haruyo (Maria) Kobayashi Hatchel and Keiko Nakamura Thurston, R.N.

I was fortunate in locating Allen A. Feitelberg in Belmont, California and Julius I. Krupp, Skokie, Illinois who "did time" with me in the 14th Signal at Kodiak. Each of these fellows dredged up long-forgotten recollections and loaned photographs which have contributed to the readability of this book. Their interest and friendly help is graciously acknowledged.

The fascinating account of the Kingfisher (OS2U) aircraft during the *Aleutian Headache,* including the search for Japanese sub *I-180* not far from Kodiak, shows that while the larger planes made the headlines, these scout-craft had jobs too. I appreciate the helpfulness of James W. Spencer, one of the pilots, who detailed the role of this little-known aircraft to me.

It is appropriate to name Donald D. McArthur of Aberdeen, Washington who is a true buff about the Japanese side of the Pacific War. Don has a large library, many artifacts as well as photographs, which he has willingly shared with us. We thank him for his friendliness and willingness to let us bounce questions against his keen knowledge.

My wife, Margie Webber, is a champion helper in every respect and I thank her warmly. She also wields a wicked blue editing pencil, reviews the flow of the language and keeps refueling the author with food.

There may be numbers of others over the several years span of assembling data for this book whose names might have been missed. If this is true, we ask forgiveness for any omissions. They were not intentional.

The author will welcome constructive criticism which should be sent in care of the publisher listed on page iv.

Bert Webber
Central Point, Oregon
Winter 1992-1993

Chapter 1
Getting Ready

Attention to the Aleutian Islands by the American government had nearly always taken a back seat when it came to showing any interest, such as providing money for expeditions of explorers, until mere months before the start of the Pacific War. But after the seizure of Attu and Kiska by the Japanese in 1942, money flowed down the Aleutian chain like oil from an uncapped well. Although history shows that the Americans won, it could be called a "near miss" of being too little, too late.

A unique ship-to-ship battle during the Pacific War would be a part of the Aleutian campaign – an Admiral would get fired over it – the Battle of the Komondorskis.

Much of Alaska, and all of the Aleutians, had never been mapped with any accuracy. Alaska had a 34,000-mile long coast-line, mostly unexplored. Ancient maps from the old Russian fur trading mission were around but these had errors so gross that neither the Americans nor Japanese could depend upon them.

During the 1930's, Japanese fishermen were rumored to be photographing all of the U.S. west coast shore lines including Alaska. But if this was true, there were significant gaps in their intelligence because some submarine skippers were directed to do this reconnaissance after the war started.

It was earlier mentioned that in 1931 a "watch-service" was openly maintained in the Western Aleutians by the Japanese who created a unique ruse to cover their presence. A Tokyo newspaper, the *Hochi-Shimbun,* promoted a so-called "good-will" flight of a single-engine airplane from Tokyo to San Francisco. In order to provide emergency fuel and food should the pilot be forced down in the Aleutians, a group of "college boys" were sent in a large "*Maru*" then dropped off at various locations in the outer islands. This was officially called the "watch-service." But Frank Dufresne, an official with the Alaska Game Commission, discovered them, talked with some of them, and noted their activity of photographing and sketching, and sounding the harbors at Attu and other places as far east as Unalaska.. Dufresne sent a written report of this "watch-service" to Washington, D.C. along with his fish and wildlife reports offering to testify in person, if asked. He wrote that he was never called. DuFresne reported that at the end of the summer, the "good-will" flight was called off so the *"Maru"* picked up all the boys and everybody went back to Japan – with pictures, sketches of harbors and mountains and with a lists of harbor soundings. He wrote that when the Japanese landed at Attu and Kiska they knew right where to go.

(During interrogation of Japanese officers after the war, Admiral Russell learned there had been some reluctance of the Japanese High Command to pursue the plan for occupying Kiska on the belief that Kiska Harbor froze in winter. Of course not. The sea south of the "line" between the Pacific Ocean and the Bering Sea is "heated" by the extension of the warm *Kuroshio* or Japanese current therefore there has never been any risk of Kiska Harbor freezing.)

What little was known about Aleutian weather could be summed up with one word: bad! Without a doubt, the three most challenging issues for the Americans and the Japanese would be the weather: Oh, the weather! The weather – mercy! As we shall see, the foggy weather caused serious collisions for warships of each navy.

But there would be other matters of grave concern including commanders who wanted more than anything to conduct the war in their own way. This caused severe interservice rivalry. As we shall see, an American admiral and an American general were "relieved from duty" – fired!

Simon Bolivar Buckner Jr. was a "front line soldier" who insisted on knowing what was going on. He wanted to make decisions based on careful planning from a hand-picked staff that could be depended upon to perform. He was not an "armchair" officer. He was a "do it now" man. While still a Colonel, Buckner had been sent to Alaska in the summer of 1940 by his immediate superior, Lt. General John L. DeWitt, Commander of the Western Defense Command and Fourth Army at the Presidio of San

Generals Simon Boliver Buckner (left) and John Lesne DeWitt were responsible for Alaska's Army preparedness and implementation program.

Francisco.

Alaska was a part of the Western Defense Command and would become that command's only active, fire-fighting theater. Buckner hadn't been in Alaska very long before he told DeWitt there were no military communications, no defenses other than armed civilians (and the 800 troops Buckner had brought with him), not even *one* Air Corps plane and no landing field if a plane had shown up!

A. C. S.

The Alaska Communications System, run by the Army Signal Corps, had an earlier title, the Washington-Alaska Military Cable and Telegraph System, "WAMCATS" for short. The service dated from 1904. It offered basic "Western Union" type dot-and-dash telegraph (later by radio), for businesses and others who paid fees for the service. Stations throughout Alaska "worked" each other plus messages to and from Alaska were routed through headquarters in Seattle. Messages for destinations beyond Seattle were switched to Western Union and Postal Telegraph Companies in Seattle. The military buildup clogged the ACS facilities forcing ACS to modernize and expand. As new military bases were opened during the expansion in the Aleutians, the Alaska Communications System went right along and on Kiska, as an example, landed with equipment to set up shop on D+2.

As to artillery in prewar Alaska, there was indeed artillery: one old Russian cannon from before 1867 and it was used only for a flower pot!

The Aleutians were strategically placed and could used by the east or the west as a jumping off place by either belligerent to the other's front door. In a presentation before the House of Representatives Committee on Military Affairs, General "Billy" Mitchell charged that the holder of Alaska held the world, that Alaska was:

the key point of the whole Pacific.... Alaska is the most strategic place in the world. It is the jumping off place to smash Japan.

As early as 1937, Alaska's Anthony Dimond had assertively reminded Congress that Alaska was without defenses. Congress appropriated money year after year for Alaska and year after year the Congress failed to release it. Instead, funds went to Panama and to Hawaii because the military had convinced Congress those locations were more important.

Meanwhile in Washington, the House had a committee for exploring Un-American activities – looking for Communists. In April 1940, a story passed over news wires about an alleged joint Russian-German venture that was building a string of submarine and air bases just 150 miles from Nome on East Cape, Siberia. The report included as "fact" that some of these Nazi-Soviet bases were on the U.S.S.R.'s Big Diomede Island. That's just 3 miles from Alaska's Little Diomede Island. As it turned out, the Germans were not involved and all the Russians were doing was building a weather station. The Diomede Islands have no harbors. Even on the larger of the two, there was no space for an air base.

Governor Ernest Gruening and General Buckner met and had a talk about the Russians and their project. They concluded that the wire services writers had done them a favor by circulating the wild and untrue story. This time Buckner kept his mouth shut and left it to Gruening. It wasn't long before Congress opened its purse and handed out more than $350 million for military construction in Alaska. Buckner got his first airplane, an obsolete Martin B-10, on August 12, 1940, when the twin-engine bomber half-skidded to a stop on the grass of Anchorage's little civilian airport. It was a beginning.

Admiral Robert A. Theobold, USN headed the "Naval presence" from Kodiak and from cruiser *Nashville*.

In Alaska, the U.S. Navy had less history than the Army. In the mid-1930's, some maneuvers had been held off the Aleutians and there were occasional visits by destroyers and submarines to various ports. But the Navy's attention to Alaska did not really start until Congress handed over the cash for construction. Three major naval bases were on the drawing boards. There would be one each for Sitka, Kodiak and Dutch Harbor. To keep things even, the Army would have cantonments at each.

The Navy would make the installation on Kodiak Island at Woman's Bay its major effort. It would soon be the base of operations for Rear Admiral Robert A. "Fuzzy" Theobald.

Theobald had been a destroyer man and was tapped by Admiral Chester W. Nimitz to carry the flag and head a small showing of the U.S. Navy in Alaskan waters. Nimitz felt there was risk that the Japanese would make landings either in the far-flung Aleutians or on Kamchatka if for no other reason than to try to stop the now daily stream of lend-lease flights of war planes going from Alaska to Siberia. A U.S. Naval presence "up north" should indicate to the Japanese they would not have a "free" time should they plan any movements in that direction.

Admiral Theobald would like a command like this. He was assigned five cruisers, four destroyers, and shortly would get half-a-dozen S-class old but very serviceable submarines. He hoisted his flag on U. S. S. *Nashville* (CL-43), a Brooklyn-class light cruiser that had been commissioned in June of 1938. But his joy with a new command wouldn't keep him happy very long.

Theobald was sour of disposition and portly of stature. He had a well known nickname: "Fuzzy." He made his own decisions and did not like interference from other quarters. Once he was on his way between Pearl and Kodiak, he received a string of messages from Nimitz. One of them told him to:

BE GOVERNED BY THE PRINCIPLE OF CALCULATED RISK

In other words, Nimitz was telling Admiral Theobald to sacrifice himself and his ships if such action was necessary to stop the Japanese from occupying any part of the coast of Alaska. Admiral Nimitz, with the help of his code breaker, Lt. Commander Joseph J. Rochefort, had determined that the major Japanese thrust in the Eastern Pacific would be Midway Island. Nimitz warned Theobald that a substantial Japanese Task Force with *two aircraft carriers* was headed his way.

"Fuzzy" fussed, fumed, fretted then messaged Nimitz:

PLANES ALONE CAN ASSURE TACTICAL RESULTS

But Nimitz had no carriers to spare.

(In the meantime, Buckner had been promoted to Brig. General, and soon upward to Major General.)

Admiral Theobald was a smart man having been very close to the top of his 1907 class at Annapolis. But under pressure, he often became terse and sometimes insulting to subordinates. When he got to Kodiak, he immediately took his flag to the brand new offices on Woman's Bay. It should be pointed out that all U.S. and Canadian Naval forces in Alaskan waters came under his command as well as American air forces in Alaska. But he had no say whatsoever over the Army – strong man Simon Bolivar Buckner Jr. – who had spent the last two years building an *offensive* system out of his Alaska *Defense* Command. Buckner was peeved at the loss of his air arm to the *Navy!*

The personality of Buckner, strong, efficient, assertive yet friendly, clashed on the very first meeting with Theobald. During a map study of the Aleutians, Buckner railed at the Admiral to "nail those damned maps up on the wall" as the large charts had been continually falling off the table onto the floor. After a heated exchange with Buckner, during which the Admiral did his best to assert that the war in the Aleutians was a Navy matter. Buckner would never agree to such a declaration so Theobald sent a message to Nimitz to clarify the roles of the two commanders. Admiral Nimitz defined the situation promptly. He directed that the relationship between the Alaska Defense Command and the Navy

IS TO BE MUTUAL COOPERATION

Theobald smarted!

The two leaders would never achieve friendship and never any such thing as "mutual cooperation." (The joint cooperation would come at much lower levels where the two services worked closely together because the enemy was shooting at them.)

General Buckner was a believer in communications and he trusted the code breakers and Admiral Nimitz to "give it to us straight." Buckner had alerted his forces on May 15th at the first report that Rochefort was certain the Japanese had attack plans in the making. The General's Dutch Harbor forces would be alert.

On the other hand, Theobald would not accept the prediction of a Japanese attack on the Navy's new base at Dutch Harbor regardless of what phraseology Nimitz used to advise him. Admiral Theobald worried a lot and decided to carry on "his" war with the Japanese in his own way.

With his small fleet, including submarines, and PBY Catalina flying boats, he would mount a picket line and when the enemy was seen, anywhere along the line, American bombers and his bigger ships could intercept and destroy them. Excellent theory so he believed.

Buckner promptly pointed out Theobold's text-book plan might sound good but *not in the Aleutians*. The distance alone was astonishing being over 1,200 miles in the islands and over 2,000 miles from Anchorage, the territory's primary base for bombers.

But the major drawback has already been mentioned: the weather! For picket boats to be effective they have to report what they *see*. If the weather is bad and one can't *see*, even if there was a major battle fleet dead-ahead, if it is not *seen* then that fleet would go unreported. As we shall learn, that is what happened. None of Theobald's submarines or picket boats had RADAR. But

The government depended on the Consolidated PBY-Catalina flying boat for news of what was going on in the Aleutians in the early days of the war. PBY was sturdy, efficient, plodding patrol bomber that became a dive-bomber during the Kiska Blitz.

Admiral Theobald would not back down. He ordered the full deployment.

The six First World War 4-stack destroyers, part of the picket line, were directed to proceed from Kodiak only as far as Dutch Harbor and were to stay there to shoot up any Japanese ships that tried to make any landings there. Theobald flatly refused to risk his cruisers anywhere near any Japanese carriers.

From his office at Kodiak, he took his flag back to *Nashville* to await developments from a position at sea several hundred miles south of Kodiak. He was 500 miles from Dutch Harbor and required his skippers maintain strict radio silence! If the Japanese brought in carriers, Theobald would be so far away it would indeed be up to the Army bombers to get them.

The 11th Air Force, commanded by Brig. General William O. Butler, had only four long-range bombers! There were also 18, B-18s, an obsolete bomber version of the famous Douglas DC-3 twin-engine transport. There were 31 factory new "Marauder" B-26 medium bombers. He also had received a few P-40 fighters and some obsolete P-36 "pursuit" planes.

Morison, on reporting aircraft strength wrote:

12 F4F [Grumman "Wildcat" carrier-type fighters] were flown up from the escort carrier *Copahee* at Seattle to Kodiak.*

None of General Butler's crews and none of the Navy's Gruman pilots had even a single combat mission and were surely no match for deadly, experienced, Zero fighter pilots.

On a late fall 1941 Sunday, services at Kodiak's Community Baptist Church were interrupted with a zoom of an airplane just over the rooftop. People rushed outdoors to see one of the P-36's spiraling upwards having just "bombed" the village with leaflets. The author picked up one of them but today does not remember what it said.

We must say here that as early as the summer of 1941, numbers of PBY Catalina flying boats – slow, long-range patrol bombers – had been patrolling Aleutian skies in good weather,

---

*Morison, Vol IV. p. 180n. According to *Jane's All the World's Aircraft 1943-44*, p. 199c, the F4F had a maximum range of 1,150 miles at cruising speed 297 mph at 19,500 ft. alt.. But the distance between Seattle and Kodiak exceeds this. Morison may have meant that the *Copahee* was somewhere at sea "off Seattle." Further, Seattle is about 100 miles inland from the sea.

when there was any, and in bad weather as a matter of habit.

Theobald knew there were two new *Top Secret* air bases but General Butler apparently had not told him they weren't ready: One was at Cold Bay, nearly 200 miles east of Dutch Harbor and the other was on Umnak Island, only 40 miles west of Dutch. The pilots didn't know about these fields. When the admiral found out about them, Butler argued with Theobald about the unreadiness of the bases. But the Navy won: move the airplanes to the unfinished flexible steel-matted runways without the concrete overlay, and do it *right away!* This was one of Theobald's more bolder moves.

In the meantime, the Japanese were on no vacation. Warrant

See page 33)

Japanese submarine-carried and launched E14Y1 "GLEN" spy plane that apparently, undetected, overflew Kodiak NAS.

Officer pilot Nobuo Fujita, in the "erector set" airplane (GLEN), from carrier-submarine *I-25*, had been launched east of Kodiak on May 27. Fujita climbed to 9,000 ft. altitude then he and his observer, Petty Officer Shoji Okuda, flew over Woman's Bay to spy and report any ship that might be anchored there. At that altitude they also saw picturesque snow-capped Pyramid Mountain and nearby Fort Greely, whose barracks and other buildings, all glistening in their cream-color paint, were planted in neat rows between Mt. Barometer and Lake Louise, a couple of miles west of the Navy installations.

None of the American sky watchers anywhere on Kodiak apparently saw or heard the Japanese plane. If there was a RADAR at that time, it missed it too. There was no alert from the Navy. Colonel Eugene E. Kent, (USA ret.) of Medford, Oregon, who was Signal Officer at Fort Greely at the time, told me years later that the Army was not aware of the spy flight. "If General [Charles H.] Corlett knew about it," he said, "I'm sure his staff would have been told."

Fujita went back out to sea where he rendezvoused with *I-25*. The little seaplane landed alongside, was hoisted aboard and Fujita reported to skipper Meiji Tagami that he and Okuda had seen a cruiser and a destroyer in Woman's Bay. He said there were no aircraft carriers there.

The intelligence gained by Fujita was critical to the Japanese effort. So much so that *I-26*, a submarine of identical specifications but not carrying any aircraft, had been detailed to the south of Kodiak to retrieve the GLEN should the U.S. Navy discover *I-25* and *I-25* had to abandon the pickup. A few days

Japanese *I-26* submarine was on spy mission in Aleutians then went to British Columbia and shot at Estevan Point Lighthouse.

later, the GLEN spotter plane from *I-9* repeated this mission. This GLEN was neither seen nor heard on the ground either.

(The author was a Signal Corps telephone switchboard operator in Kent's command and at this time was on loan to the Navy to run their automatic telephone switchboard. Most telephone operators "tin-eared" calls at night as calls were few and there was nothing else to do. I, and my friends on the army's old-style non-dial boards, heard nothing about any enemy airplanes having been over the American bases on Kodiak.)

The weather at the bases in the Aleutians has to be experienced to be believed. "Williwaws," freakish winds that whip up on short notice and roar through the canyons between volcano peaks on the islands, damp air so thick that it plugs aircraft carburetors and ice that forms on wings to the degree that a plane can't take off, were of great concern. Just keeping men's feet from freezing and their fingers flexible enough to operate equipment was a challenge in itself.

In spite of the weather, the patrols ordered by Admiral Theobald were to be made. The subject was not one for discussion. That was all there was to it. Bomber Command had an extraordinary commander, Colonel William O. Eareckson, and the Navy had Captain Leslie E. Gehres. Between them, they kept aircraft in the air on a daily basis, "williwaws" or not. Each group had a patrol pattern to fly. The 36th Bomb Squadron had an old B-17 called "Old Seventy" which, from its base on the unfinished Umnak runway, took to the air every day. The B-17 airplane, all four engines of it, can stay aloft for a long time but it's expensive to fuel and can only set down if there is *terra firma* under it. PBY'S, the early versions, could land only on water. But the newer amphibian model (PBY5A), once it became available, could stay up about 24 hours and carry a large load of bombs. But the "P-boat" as it was affectionately called, had a cruising speed of only 95 knots which was an immediate indicator to some that the best duty for these ungainly craft would be for routine patrols and search and rescue missions. The Navy would learn more about PBY's hidden charm capabilities in due time.

Of the heavy bombers, it will be recalled there were four. Two were the prototype B-17's and the other two were LB-30 's. These

Lt. Cdr. James S. Russell (left), Commanding officer of Navy Patrol Squadron VP-42, piloted actor-comedian Joe E. Brown (center) to Dutch Harbor in PBY5A. Brown had been guest of General Charles H. Corlett, (right) Commander of Fort Greely where actor entertained troops.

aircraft had been fitted out for the British, but under the skin they were B-24's.

Communications throughout Alaska had always been a challenge mostly because of distance and sparse settlement. But "challenge" was a polite word for real trouble. The Army and Air Force operated on different radio frequencies and these were separate from the Navy's. None of the radios were "balanced," or standardized, having been "scrounged" from various sources. Some were home made. A few of the better radios were purchased from individuals. One incident was the pressure put upon a Signal Corps buck private who was assertively promoted to sell his mail-order Hallicrafter SX-28 to the Army.

To top off this ludicrous arrangement, there was a critical shortage of Army men who could send messages by Morse Code—"brass pounders" they were called—which meant many messages over short distances had to be transmitted in s-l-o-w oral, phonetics which were subject to great error, as well as

31

becoming a give-away of the message's content to any enemy that might be listening. With a battle, or at least an enemy attack about to be rained down upon them, the Aleutian islands were without the most important item of war: suitable communications.

The Aleutians, really a string of volcanoes, were about to see eruptions not of hot lava but of another kind: bombs, torpedoes, bullets. Among the American military, all of the bosses were well out of range. Theobald was sitting it out on *Nashville* under radio silence hundreds of miles away. Both Generals Butler, Air Force, and General Buckner, Army, were in their headquarters at Anchorage 800 miles from Dutch Harbor where the first eruption would happen.

But field commanders were alert and ready for anything that came their way. Lt. Commander James S. "Jim" Russell was boss of PBY Squadron 42. He and Eareckson had become good friends. And there was Col. Norman D. Sillen, an Air Force fighter man.

Here is a good place to remind that on Theobald's first day at

Colonel William Eareckson was valiant leader in Air Force who assertively "bombed hell out of Japanese" on Kiska

Kodiak, he and General Buckner had not done very well in what is known as interpersonal relations, and their immediate junior staffs had quickly taken the sides of each commander. There were complaints of non-communication at this upper level that were so urgent that messages were sent "down line" directing the services to cooperate.

Jim Russell, who retired as a an Admiral, gave me this anecdote during one of several personal interviews about inter-service cooperation:

> Eareckson and I needed to know what was going on and needed to be in instant reach of each other, so we arranged to bunk together at Cold Bay. We put our bunks in the Navy radio tent. My feet were nearest the radioman. If the radio brought something we needed to know, the radioman would shake my foot and in turn would wake Eareckson who was next to me. This way both of us could get much-needed sleep yet be ready instantly if duty called.

Commander Russell had been flying the "chain" for over one year and had the place pretty well in his head. He had hauled General Buckner down to Dutch and had done inspection patrols all the way to Attu. His PBY's were armed to the teeth, manned with trigger-ready crews and always kept fueled. They flew long, tiring, weather-fighting patrols daily. It would be one of these long range P-boats that would radio the first alert, about noon on June 2, that an enemy fleet was on the way. Although the weather over all the Aleutians was nothing less than atrocious, two PBY's were alerted to make further investigation and managed to get into the air about dark. They rumbled through the storm, never got out of it, and never saw the enemy.

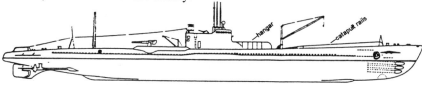

I-15-Class Submarines. (Pictures on pages 28, 29)
Type B-1, 108 meters long, crew 100+ including 1 pilot and 1 observer-navigator for GLEN aircraft. The Japanese had 44 aircraft-carrying submarines of which 9 were sinking ships off the U.S. West Coast within 10 days after the attack on Pearl Harbor. For the complete account of the activities of these vessels and the aircraft, one of which dropped bombs and started a forest fire in Oregon, see *Silent Siege-III; Japanese Attacks on North America in WW-II, Ships Sunk, Air raids, Bombs Dropped, People Killed.*

Insignia (clockwise) 11th Air Force; Alaska Defense Command; soldier who earned these "hash-marks" had 2½-years foreign service; Corlett's "long-knives" Kiska liberators; Unofficial Alaska Defense Command patch.

Chapter 2
"ABOUT TO BE BOMBED BY ENEMY PLANES"
The Dutch Harbor Raids

At sea, Admiral Theobald had a restless night. The storm tossed his ships in all directions and any resemblance to maintaining a picket line was only in his dreams. During the storm, Admiral Kakuji Kaktua's Aleutian Task Force passed through the pickets undetected.

On May 5, Japanese Imperial Headquarters published an order authorizing a sweeping naval operation against Midway and the Aleutians. The flagship of the Aleutians-bound Imperial force was aircraft carrier *Ryujo* (Captain Tadao Kato), with Rear Admiral Kakuji Kakuta, Task Force Commander, aboard. Lt. Commander Masatake Okumiya was Flight Operations Officer.

A second carrier, *Junyo*, raced along about three-quarters-of-a-mile away. Between these two light carriers were 82 airplanes. For protection there were the heavy cruisers *Maya* and *Takao* and three destroyers followed by an oiler. The reinforcements, not far behind, were cruisers, *Abukuma, Kiso, Nachi* and *Tama,* plus nine destroyers shepherding three transports into which 2,500 invasion troops of the Imperial Army were crammed. There were heavy cruiser *Nachi* plus two supporting destroyers, near Paramushiro (the northernmost island of the Kuriles) where Vice Admiral Boshiro Hosogaya, overall operation commander, hoisted his flag. In addition, there was an advance force consisting of six I-class aircraft carrier submarines pushing through the awful weather on the lookout for any potential seaborne opposition These were the: *I-9, I-15, I-17, I-19, I-25, I-26.* Of this group only *I-26* did not have an airplane on board.

The weather was normal: foggy. The Japanese plan was to bomb Dutch Harbor then to invade Adak, Attu and Kiska.

We recall that on June 2, a lone PBY on patrol spotted the carriers and immediately radioed an alert. Around 3 a.m. on June

(Left page) Imperial submarine *I-26* on patrol. Note rails of airplane catapult in center view. *I-26* did not carry a plane during war but used hangar for cargo. (This page) Submarine *I-10* leaving Yokosuka for pre-Pearl-Harbor attack patrol that saw it on station off San Diego, California in mid-December 1941.

Vice Admiral Hosogaya, Imperial Japanese Navy, was a key player in the Aleutians

3, the Japanese carriers were about 180 miles southwest of Dutch Harbor when the order was given to launch the first planes. *Ryujo* put 14 attack planes and three fighters into the air and *Junyo* launched 15 bombers along with 13 fighters. These 45 planes headed for the target. Alas, all of *Junyo's* raiders got lost in the fog and had to go back to the ship. Right at 8:08 a. m. the weather broke and three of *Rhuyo's* fighters and nine of the attackers spotted the installations of the Dutch Harbor Naval Base and the cream-colored two-story barracks of Fort Mears laid out below them.

The Americans at Dutch had a little warning. Seaplane tender U.S.S. *Gillis* was on the way out of port at 5:40 a.m. when her RADAR picked up lots of quick-moving pips heading in from the south above the clouds at about 10,000 feet altitude – distance about 10 miles. The ship radioed a *FLASH* message and Dutch Harbor's commander sounded *RED* alert. As sirens wailed, all ships in harbor went to battle stations and got up steam. On shore in the radio shack, the brass-pounder hit his key and a message split the morning air:

"ABOUT TO BE BOMBED BY ENEMY PLANES"

Men sprang to their weapons, regardless of their state of dress, into prepared positions as fast as they could. Everyone would not make it. By this time the attackers were over the target, led by Lt. Hiroichi Samejima in his KATE, a sleek single-engine craft which could be fitted with either bombs or torpedoes. His target was the radio shack to which he was guided by the tall antenna. Samejima's bomb missed and the radio man pounded another

(Left page) Japanese bombers have just attacked Dutch Harbor, killed soldiers, set barracks on fire. (This page) damage to civilian hospital.

Morse message:

"THAT ONE KNOCKED ME OFF MY CHAIR"

as mud and rocks peppered the shack.

Flack was bursting in the air as American gunners, both Army and Navy, started shooting. Below, a PBY "mail plane" was warming as was another Catalina. The mail plane, with two passengers aboard, was piloted by Lt. Jack Litsey and was nearly airborne when bullets from two Japanese fighters raked the clumsy plane killing both passengers and setting the craft afire. Lt. Litsey plopped the plane back into the water and ran it up on

> I remember that morning very well when the Jap first struck Dutch Harbor. I was the first man to discover the High Flying Bombers. We had a triangle-gong on the side of the Orderly Room and I pounded HELL out of it and I hollared, "The Japs was flying over" and minutes later the bombs started to fall. Our outfit didn't get hit – lucky!
> —Bruce Evans, Co. A. 37th Inf.
> Columbus, Georgia

I was on deck of the *Fillmore* when planes came over. I said to a guy that we had plenty of air cover then as we watched little things started falling out of the planes .The things were bombs and we were caught flat-footed. I came off that ship without even touching the gangplank and we took off into the hills for cover. There was never an alarm until after the attack started.

—Mack Mark, M Co. 71st Inf.
Canoga Park, California

Ken Reynolds, who liked the Navy and made a career of it was on the *Fillmore* when it was strafed at Dutch Harbor. He caught a spent bullet in his thigh but the wound did not draw blood. He was awarded the Purple Heart. —The Editor

the beach. He piled out, dashed behind some rocks just as his P-boat blew up. Ensign Hildebrand, in the second Catalina, got into the air with only part of his crew. He pulled up under a Zero which probably never saw him. His gunners, and anti-aircraft fire from below, were piling shells into the fighter which crashed into the bay.

As some attackers shot up PBY's at their buoys, others bombed the fuel storage tanks, set a 1½ ton Chevrolet Army truck afire and hit a barracks, killing 25 soldiers and wounding that many more. One bomb demolished the Russian Orthodox Church in the village. The attackers reported they had spotted the ships in harbor – none of which had made the open sea – therefore a second attack force was launched from *Rhujo* at 9:45 a.m.

Admiral Kakuta felt good about the mission thus far so this flight was made up of 14 attack planes, 15 bombers, a dozen Zero fighters and for good measure, he ordered the cruisers to catapult four observation planes whose job was to observe – not fight. But

Cap Collier, our bugler, was killed early morning June 3. He'd just finished blowing Reveille. Bomb frags tore him to pieces. I was Supply Sgt. I was with Cap about 2 minutes before the Japs bombed but we were apart about 50 yards when he got killed. A Jap Zero strafed the beach where I was and a soldier got hit about 10 feet from me. I didn't know him. The only injury I had was during the second raid on June 4. I was running for a fox hole and I fell on a rock and cut my knee. When our outfit came home, I brought Cap's battered bugle to his parents as his and my families were neighbors. But the bugle was lost in their house fire some years later.

—Oscar Jones, Hq Btry 206th CA (AA).
Tupelo, Arkansas

Newspapers from Portland, Oregon.

by this time Makushin Bay was socked in. The carrier-based planes headed back to the ship in about one hour having seen exactly nothing but became hopelessly lost in the fog.

About this time the Task Force commander was handed a message from Tokyo telling him to give Adak a raking over so invasion troops could land. But again it was a matter of weather. The soup was so thick that no run on Adak could possibly be made. The flight was called off. Eventually the whole Adak plan was scrapped thus the Japanese never did land there.

> The second day we had foxholes. Next to us was a nest in the tundra with 4 little blue eggs. Every time a Jap plane started shooting, the closest man put his helmet over the nest before we hit the foxhole.
> —Mack Mark, M Co. 71st Inf.
> Canoga Park, California

41

Virgil O. Smith, Navy radioman turned gunner at Dutch Harbor bombing

I was a radioman assigned to a gun as we were short of men. The guns came the day before the Japs hit and we installed them that day ready to fire to let the Japs know we were at home. My gun was bombed the second alert on second day. Planes came over Mt. Ballyhoo dropping bombs down the mountain side. My gun was at the foot of the mountain. I was in harness when the bomb exploded nearby. Concussion was terrific – it bend the gun barrel and armor plate. How I walked away in one piece I will never know. We didn't have any helmets. I have 80 percent VA disability for my ears.   —Virgil O. Smith, CWO-2 USN-ret.
Rogers, Arkansas

I moved into Dutch in Aug. 1, 1941 in Btry A, 206th CA (AA) Arkansas National Guard. We worked searchlights but in re-organization became a 3-inch gun battery but I went to I Btry with 90mm AA gun. In June '42 when Dutch was bombed, I was part of a RADAR unit at Humpty Cove overlooking entrance to Dutch Harbor and Bering Sea. We operated 3 RADAR units
—Don Drake, Artillery
Las Vegas, Nevada.

In Aug., Sept., Oct. '41 Jap fishing vessels were coming in [at Dutch Harbor] and we traded cigs and candy for some of their junk. We found out they were all the time sounding the harbor and taking pictures of oil storage tanks and warehouses. I had spent 18 months on Hog Island up there when I was crippled running telephone lines around the mountain and an ice and snow slide put me into ole Bering Sea – my buddy drowned.
—Sam S. Standard 206th CA (AA)
Little Rk, Arkansas

I was an army gunner assigned to various ships. On S.S. *Yukon* Alaska Steamship Co., we came in to Dutch Harbor after the bombing to pick up civilians.
—Melvin Heere. Gun Crew.
Minot N. Dakota

Our 250th Coast Artillery, Harbor Defense, was San Francisco Nat'l Guard. My B Btry got to Dutch in April 1941 to be ready. We lived on top of Mt. Ballyhoo. I was Personnel Sgt/Major.
—Frank E. Fox. Mill Valley, California

Climbing up from Uniktali Bay, Dutch Harbor, then up through Uniktali Pass was back-breaking labor but it had to be done.

The worst part of being at Dutch Harbor was the weather. We had snow, rain and sleet. The wind would blow snow down your shirt collar and up your pant legs at the same time and there were days on days when the wind never let up, sometimes 50 miles an hour. It snowed so hard you could hardly see anything. We had a gun position on top of Mt. Ballyhoo and driving up and down the mountain day and night was risky as we used no lights at all.
—Elmo W. Dalton Hq. Btry. 206th Coast Artillery
Benton, Kentucky

Alaska place names appeared on postmarks of Navy ships from about 1932 until the practice was halted apparently during summer 1942. As we saw earlier, the Navy witheld announcement of the Japanese attacks on Dutch Harbor for some time but the destroyer *Gilmer* (Lt. Cdr. Herman O. Parish, Master), was immediately advertising the attack in his postmark.

Chapter 3
Surprise From Umnak

When the *RED* alert had been sounded early that morning, the air crews at the secret American base at Cold Bay hustled into their P-40's for the 200-mile flight to Dutch Harbor. Their attitude was tense. They wanted action and knew other Americans should be there fighting Zeros, having taken off from the other secret base only *40 miles* away – Umnak. When the Cold Bay flight arrived all they met was fog and the raiders had scooted for their carrier. The disappointment was keen and itchy trigger fingers would have to wait. The P-40's went back to Cold Bay where – frustration on top of frustration – word awaited them that Umnak's squadron had never left the ground! The make-shift radio system had failed and Umnak didn't know Dutch had been raided until told of it hours later.

The Japanese had been certain there would be no American fighter opposition on the belief that American fighters were based at Kodiak well out of range. The Japanese presumed their only risk would be from anti-aircraft fire and minor irritation from PBY'S. Admiral Kakuta had lost only one plane. But he was in for a surprise!

We recall the cruisers had launched four observation planes to report on the second Dutch Harbor bombing. On their way back to their ships, all four became lost in the fog. As the bi-planes emerged from the fog they were about 40 miles west of Dutch Harbor *right over the secret Umnak base!*

Spotted from the ground, all twenty-one P-40's scrambled. While the Mitsubishi F1M2 Navy Type 0 (Allied code named PETE) observer craft looked clumsy with its biplane design, it was a formidable opponent when on equal footing. But its 230 miles-per-hour speed was no match for a P-40 which zipped through the air over 100 miles-per-hour faster. Although the PETES took evasive action one was shot down in front of cheering ground

Secret air strip on Unmak island 40 miles west of Dutch Harbor.

crewmen. A second PETE was shot up so badly it crashed into the sea. The remaining duo managed to hide in the fog and eventually got back to their cruisers.

In the Japanese "camp," heads were scratched as to where the P-40's had come from. Nevertheless, a second strike on Dutch Harbor was announced for two days later so all the Japanese efforts were bent toward that end. On June 5, Admiral Kukuta ordered "launch" for his attackers. These were 11 bombers and 11 fighters. Over the target, the weather cleared just in time for the force to see Dutch Harbor easily. The planes went for the oil storage tanks which they promptly blew up. That explosion cost Americans 750,000 gallons of fuel, 22,000 gallons just delivered a day or so earlier.

The defenses of Dutch Harbor were now being manned 24 hours a day thus the attackers met withering ground fire. Even so, none of it hit any Japanese airplanes. While the attackers strafed and bombed, there were 18 lives lost on the ground. Although Umnak radio still wasn't working, the troops there (Fort Glen) and airmen didn't need radio to announce the raid this time for when that oil tank went up the roar was so thunderous it was heard on Umnak.

The P-40's took off immediately to confront a flight of Zeros which was regrouping over the west end of Unalaska Island in sight of Umnak. Eight P-40's were in the air and almost at once a Zero was shot down. Within minutes another Zero was shot up and went "dead in the air" – crashed.

The Americans had casualties too. Lt. John J. Cape, 23, had drawn first Japanese blood that day but he was shot down minutes later. Another P-40 pilot had his engine shot out of action. On fire, Lt. Winfield E. McIntyre crash-landed on Umnak's beach but walked away from his wreck. Two more Zeros were so full of American holes they fell into the ocean before getting back to the carrier. The remaining four, now very low on fuel, observed a lone PBY below them. One of the fighter pilots made up his mind he was going to "get that plane," so he bore in on the waddling bomber and tore it apart.

Admiral James S. Russell, Col. Zenji Abe, Ted Spencer of Alaska Historical Aviation Society, Admiral Hiroichi Samejima, Col. Benjamin B. Talley made special flight from Dutch Harbor to Umnak to prove to Col. Abe that the once secret airfield really existed. Abe could still not believe it 35 years after the war.

The War Experiences of Clifford E. Johnson

NOTE: Nearly one year before Pearl Harbor, Cliff Johnson was called up with the Washington D.C. National Guard's 260th Coast Artillery (AA). The unit went to Dutch Harbor. Later he became an Infantry officer and was in the Ardennes and Rhineland campaigns where he was awarded two Purple Hearts. He was Commended for "fine work and courage while under attack" by Brig. Gen. E. B. Colladay. His story is told here as an example of similar experiences of many. —The editor.

Two days after Pearl Harbor we took a train to the Pacific Northwest in G Battery with 8, 37mm AA guns and 2, .50-cal. machine guns. We lived at the Puyallup Fair Grounds then set up to protect the Boeing Airplane plant at Seattle. In May 1942, we loaded on the *President Fillmore* for the Aleutians. Our guns were set on deck for action. Left Seattle on May 27 with a 1-destroyer escort that zigzagged in front of us every mile of the trip. We arrived at Dutch Harbor on June 2 and tied up at the wooden pier.

Around 5 a.m. on June 3, general quarters sounded. We manned our guns and saw Jap bombers hit the oil tank on shore. They also bombed and strafed our ship. The ship, which had steam up, backed out from the pier then circled until the all clear signal. The Japs bombed again on June 4 and we shot at them. The *Fillmore* was not hit and my unit suffered no casualties,

We went to Cold Bay and set up guns around the secret air strip but stayed only about 2 weeks. Next we took ship for Port Heiden where I was a corporal in Fire Control Section. The unit was renamed the 503d. We set our weapons where the engineers built an air strip. We lived in tents until Sept. when we got steel huts. An infantry outfit was also there. Water was scarce so we dug wells and we also distilled our private booze. The winter was awful cold, snowy, some days the wind was 40 - 50 mph. We were on the highest point we could find, 1 mile inland from Bering Sea which froze. Stocked a huge wood pile for emergency signal fire.

I put in for Officer's Candidate School then left Port Heiden in a C-47 for Anchorage. I sailed for Seattle on the *General Goethals* then by train to North Carolina for OCS.

Lt. Clifford Johnson went to France as a platoon commander and was in about 20 fire fights in Belgium, Luxembourg and Germany. He was wounded twice, more severely at Mainz by a mortar burst "that ended the war for me." He was discharged in Nov. 1945 after 4 years 8 months of "being a civilian out of place." Although he has always limped due to his wounds, he spent 32 years with Exxon. —The editor

Chapter 4
The "Gift" of a Zero

The single survivor of that PBY that the Zero had shot down, Aviation Machinists Mate Gunner W. H. Rawls, paddled away in a little raft. But the Japanese pilot didn't like Americans so he machine-gunned Rawls in his raft – a sad ending for Mr. Rawls who, although now dead, was about to become an unsung hero in the midst of the *Aleutian headache*..

As the Japanese pilot left the scene and headed for his carrier, his eye caught his oil-pressure gauge just as the needle descended rapidly to "0." He radioed the carrier in plain language of his plight and asked for the submarine to fetch him. He was now over Akutan Island, east of Unalaska and decided to set down there.

All pilots know that a landing, regardless of how rough it might be, is called a good landing if one can walk away from it. The Japanese pilot lowered his landing gear as he neared the island. Unschooled in Alaska land-based flying, he didn't realize that when his wheels touched the boggy tundra the plane would instantly stop. As the wheels hit they were locked in the tundra and the air-plane flipped upside down. The whip-lash snapped the pilot's neck. He died quickly. Japanese pilots saw the wreck but for their own reasons wrote it off. About a month later, the upside down Zero was discovered by an inquisitive PBY crew on a routine patrol

When a U.S. Navy investigation crew landed following the P-boat's message, they saw but a single bullet hole in the crashed Zero. Gunner Rawls had knicked only the pressure gauge indicator line. The airplane was otherwise in near-perfect shape. The Zero's pilot, Flight Petty Officer Tadayoshi Koga, in his insistence of boring in on Rawls' PBY, took Rawls' life needlessly but in losing his own had delivered into U.S. hands the first Zero fighter plane to be recovered virtually intact. With high priority, the Zero was carefully picked up then carried on a U.S. Navy gunboat directly to the States.

Mitsubishi's famous Zero-*sen* fighter plane that crashed on Akutan after a raid on Dutch Harbor. Damage to plane was slight.

Jiro Horikoshi, the engineer to whom credit for the invention of the Japanese mystery fighter (*Mitsubishi Zero-sen*), wrote:

> An almost undamaged Zero made a forced landing [in the Aleutians] and the United States took possession of it. There was not a single person in Japan at the time who knew this. Now the Americans were able to investigate Japan's newest fighter from all angles [and] flight tests. [This] was an unfortunate incident [for Japan].

The Captured Zero Fighter

The research on the part of the Americans started with a careful study in California to see how this airplane was built then it was repaired. Next, this Japanese fighter plane was given U.S. markings then was test flown alongside several American fighter planes to determine specifically the plus and minus points of each when compared with each of the others. As a result of the study, aircraft designers produced a fighter plane specifically to outfly and outfight the Zero. This was the Grumman F6F "Hellcat."

Chapter 5
Chasing the Japanese

Right after the first attack on Dutch Harbor, Eareckson's bombers had taken to the air in search of the Japanese Task Force. One of the inter-service collaborations between Navy's Commander Russell and the Air Force, was to teach the B-26 boys how to rig and drop Navy torpedoes. One B-26, so fixed, discovered both carriers through a hole in the clouds and roared in for the kill. Just as he let go his torpedo, the pitching and stormy sea rolled the *Rhujo* and the torpedo went over the carrier's deck and crashed into the sea where it exploded well clear of the ship. The B-26 pilot, Air Force Captain George "Wayne" Thornbrough, who was the Operations Officer of the 73rd Bomber Squadron, only wanted to get back to base, rearm and head out again now that he knew where the carriers were. On landing at Cold Bay, the pilot gave a complete description and location of the Japanese to Commander Russell who raced to the radio shack to alert the other commands. Thornbrough was back in the air quickly but his luck had run out. Near midnight, he radioed his position and the signal was picked up at Cold Bay. Commander Russell, with the seaplane tender *Casco's* direction finder, tried to talk down the B-26. The pilot was trying to land on the radio signal when he crashed about 40 miles out. The crew did not survive.

The B-17's had RADAR and set out from Umnak to find the carriers. "Old-70" dropped bombs from low altitude – all missed. The second Fortress went in at even lower level and headed for *Takao* but the bomber was totally obliterated by flack bursts. The wreckage crashed clear of the cruiser. No one got out.

From the Navy side, Lt. Charles E. "Cy" Perkins took a PBY on a search for the carriers. With RADAR he found his targets and with two 500-pound bombs, plus a torpedo, he radioed that he was closing on the enemy. While the P-boats were never intended to be dive bombers, the pilots in the Aleutians learned the tricks of this trade. "Cy" put his P-boat into a dive, leveled off at the deck and headed straight for *Junyo*. But *Junyo's* guns shot up his starboard engine and Perkins had his hands full just trying to keep the plane in the air. He had to drop his munitions into the sea along with much of his fuel in order to get back to the base on one engine. For his valor, Perkins received a Navy Cross.

Earlier, Wylie M. Hunt, a Navy Lieutenant (jg) flying co-pilot with Lt. (jg) Gene Cusick in a PBY out of Umnak, got in the way of a patrol of Zeros from *Junyo*. The Catalina didn't last long. The Zeros, now code named "ZEKE," shot out an engine and set one wing on fire. Cusick, wounded, and Hunt put the flying boat down onto the sea. Of the crew, only Hunt and two enlisted men survived the landing and drift in the small raft in freezing weather. In time, *Takao* sighted them and took them aboard. The men were separated immediately. Hunt, on the second day, was roughed up by a returning pilot who had been jumped by American fighters from the secret Umnak base.

Japanese briefing officers threatened Hunt with death if he didn't reveal all. Hunt kept his mouth shut. Japanese weighted his body, had him "walk a plank" to the edge, then jerked a blindfold off his head for one final query about the airfield. Hunt, who had flown from there still pleaded ignorance. His captors believed him, kept him on *Takao* another three weeks, then sent him to a prison camp in Japan.

*   *   *

We will recall that earlier plans called for the Japanese to take Adak Island by invasion right after the air raid on Dutch Harbor. They saw that the weather was its usual 'bad," thus the pre-invasion bombardment was called off. Admiral Hosogaya, sitting it out in *Nachi*, was distressed to learn of the secret base on Umnak. Aware that this closeness to American bombers would be a menace to life for any Japanese on Adak – only 250 miles away – Hosogaya scratched the planned occupation of Adak from his invasion outline and notified Admiral Yamamoto.

With this episode behind them, the Dutch Harbor attack force turned west to join with Admiral Hosogawa's group. Together they approached Attu, again passing through Theobald's pickets undetected.

In the states, newspapers headlined the Japanese bombing at Dutch Harbor on June 4th, then on the 20th set block headline type reading:

NAVY DENIES ALEUTIAN RAID

News of the Japanese losses at Midway brought cheers to the Americans in Alaska and especially at Dutch Harbor. While Admiral Kakuta was miserable for the plight of Imperial Navy's debacle at Midway, he was satisfied with his own performance in the north.

The box score of the two sides after the Dutch Harbor attacks was uneven:

	United States	Japan
Dead	78	15
Aircraft lost	14	11
Prisoners taken	0	3

American anti-aircraft guns fired over 12,000 rounds from ground positions plus about that much more from ships in harbor. All combined, and with help from the gunners on a PBY, this tremendous firepower shot down exactly one enemy plane.

On a cold night one of the men left the poker game to return to his own hut. It was the rule to use the field phone to call his hut when a man was returning alone at night. After about an hour he had not returned so the Battery was alerted to look for him. He was finally found lying on the edge of the runway. His elbow-length fur gauntlets had fallen off. His hands were frozen. The medics saved his hands but he lost all his fingernails and skin.

—(Name withheld by request) Cold Bay

When we were wrecked on Sanak Island we thought we'd have a nice Christmas dinner as there were a lot of ducks on the bay. We managed to shoot some but while they were cooking they smelled so bad of fish we couldn't eat them. We had C rations instead: beans, beef stew, corned beef hash. I spent 28 months in the chain.

—Robert G. White, B Co. 42nd Engrs.
W. Sacramento, California

Nazan Bay – Atka
The Navy's Favorite Harbor For
Its Seaplane Tenders

Admiral Jim Russell identified this photograph in these words:

U.S.S. *Gillis,* a destroyer that had been converted into a seaplane tender, is tending PBYs that can be seen at buoys inshore of her. Knowing our temporary base had been discovered, Lt. Cdr. Garton, C.O. of *Gillis,* embarked the Aleuts from Atka Village and retired to Dutch Harbor with *Gillis.* Kawanishi (MAVIS) flying boats from Kiska bombed the village the next day. I walked over the area later – bomb craters shorts and overs – *no* direct hits! I found this reconnaissance photograph in Japan.

⭕ PBYs at buoys planted by *Gillis*   Atka village to left beyond ✕

Chapter 6
Where Do We Go From Here?

General Buckner ordered some reorganizational plans forthwith. One of his first was to revamp communications. Detachments of a number of existing outfits were formed to move to extended positions with their equipment. Among the units affected was the 14th Signal Service Company at Fort Greely which was directed to make its "contribution." These units provided "brasspounding" code men, radio repairmen, telephone installers and "grunts" (helpers) as well as for other tasks.

Sergeant Sammy Mahar, an old-time Regular Army Signal Corps brass-pounder, was shipped (with a smuggled 5th of bourbon) to Cold Bay. Master Sergeant and Wire Chief Les Mordick growled at being sent to Dutch thence to Adak. Pfc Julius I. Krupp, a telephone operator, was a licensed "ham" who also held a commercial radio ticket. He had been spending every extra minute practicing Morse Code with a mechanical sending kit to keep up his skills. He went to Afognak Island as a radioman to set up communications with a logging company that was milling rough lumber under contract with the Army.

The 14th Signal unit at Kodiak also saw two members, Sgt Joe Morrison and Corporal Dale Ramm go off to Officer's Candidate School in the states. A young Sergeant of the 215th Coast Artillery (AA) also went to OCS to be returned after 90 days as a 2nd Lieutenant. (He was immediately assigned to Quartermaster Corps as the fort's garbage control officer.)

In the Fort Greely Headquarters was Sergeant Robert G. Lindemuth, a displaced Finance Dept. accountant. He worked in the Provost Marshall's office and was, among other tasks to the dismay of many an old soldier, in charge of opening confiscated bottles of whiskey and pouring the contends into a toilet. Moved to Amchitka, Lindemuth went back to computing unit payrolls.

Japanese Navy Landing party occupies Kiska which they named
Narukami-shima. American Navy weather men (lower) captured
on Kiska were taken to prison camps in Japan. Dog, "Explosion,"
survived occupation and was liberated by American troops.

Chapter 7
Japanese on Kiska* and Attu

Admiral Theobald, still at sea on *Nashville,* was having difficulty containing himself. Theobald, itching for action, ordered the Commanding Officer of *Nashville* to leave the rest of the ships and get to Kodiak at top speed as one of Gehres' RADAR-equipped PBY's had reported what was believed to be aircraft carriers and escorts in the Bering Sea.

In reaction, Theobald directed there be an intensive air/sea search. He went back to *Nashville* which was waiting with steam up, put to sea and churned water heading into the west.

At the Battle of Midway, Admiral Yamamoto lost four of his major carriers and a cruiser as well as thousands of men including most of his best pilots. He had failed in his all-out effort to subdue the U. S. fleet and he would not have another chance on such a grand scale. Although he retired from Midway in shambles, he had achieved a small victory – sort of – in the Aleutians. His forces there had taken three islands of North American soil. His High Command heralded this as a great victory but did not tell the Japanese people of the debacle at Midway. Admiral Yamamoto did not realize at the time of his seizure of Kiska, Attu and Agattu that the occupation of these islands would become like opening of a can of worms for him.

*   *   *

Captain Takeji Ono, Imperial Japanese Navy, landed on Kiska a little after 1 a.m. on June 7th, with special Navy landing troops.

---

*Why Kiska? The initial Japanese eastern line of observation for a chance attack on its home islands was a line of picket ships about 800 miles at sea. This was the line that the Halsey-Doolittle Raid of April 18th stumbled on when Colonel James H. Doolittle had led his flight of 16 B-25B bombers from the carrier *Hornet* for the attacks on Japan. Because of the success of the Doolittle Raid, the Japanese High Command could see this picket line was ineffective because it was not out far enough so planned a farther and greater line. Kiska was to be the northern outpost. Midway Island was to be in the center and Samoa was on the southern end. The Japanese traumatic defeat at Midway scuttled the plan. The Japanese landed and seized Kiska but never did land on Samoa.

He was followed by over 1,000 infantry. Within a short time, the advance men reached the American's Navy's radio shack which was manned by ten men. The U.S. Navy needed the weather information from Kiska and had, just days earlier, brought in new equipment and supplies. The men were awakened by the shattering of their hut by Japanese machine gun bullets that wounded two of the weathermen. The other eight scampered into the foggy dark along with their mascot, a dog named "Explosion."

The wounded sailors were captured, given medical attention, then declared to be prisoners of war. Seven others would give themselves up later when confronted by riflemen when the Americans went to their food caches which the Japanese had discovered and were watching. All were sent to Japan except for one William House. He had sneaked away from the others and hid in a cave to await for an American counterattack which did not come. In the meantime, he ate whatever he could find including grass. He lost much weight because of lack of nourishment. Finally, unable to hold out any longer, he gave himself up after *fifty days* in the cold. His captors were amazed at his stamina, fed him and cared for him until he was well enough to be sent to Japan as a prisoner.

On the same morning as the landing on Kiska, another Japanese force landed at Massacre Bay on Attu. Within hours, the forces on both Kiska and Attu numbered about 1,250 men on each island.

The 41 people on Attu were 39 natives and the American school teacher and his wife. Of the native Aleuts, about half were children. Teacher and radio operator Foster Jones, 60, was gunned down by the invaders as he raced toward his prepared hideout on a hill above the village. His wife and the Aleuts were interned in Japan for the rest of the war.

While the Japanese of Admiral Hosogaya's Northern Force were busy landing and digging in on Kiska and Attu, "Fuzzy" Theobald was still churning water in the Bering Sea looking for a non-existent enemy fleet. Again, the American admiral missed the action.

General Buckner had been pushing General DeWitt for more airplanes for months and on the day after the second Dutch

Heavily armed P-38 Lightning fighter plane saw first combat flying in the Aleutians.

Harbor raid, a flight of shiny, factory-new, twin-engine P-38 "Lightning" fighters put down on the new Umnak airstrip.

Chapter 8
The Kiska Blitz

Through a hole in the fog, one of the LB-30's spotted ships at anchor in Kiska harbor but couldn't identify them. By the time he got back to Umnak and described the ships to an Intelligence Officer, a PBY radioman was pounding his transmitting key telling Umnak that the PBY was then over Kiska and a Japanese fleet was in the harbor.

The enemy had been located. What to do? The decisions were up to the top command – Washington, D.C. These were the considerations:

     1.) Congress didn't want Japanese sitting on American soil.

     2.) The various branches of the services had their own reasons for either leaving the Japanese there to freeze or to drive them off.

     3.) President Roosevelt just wanted to end the war as quickly as possible.

Captured Japanese film.
Staff Officers and tank
with crew on Kiska.
Navy photographer
made post cards and
distributed them to
the men.

A JAPANESE TANK CREW ON KISKA

Unidentified Japanese officers at Narukami-shima (Kiska) seen on film found there by U. S. Navy

All the confab was quickly congealed into a single order: *Get Kiska back!* It would take time.

On June 11, a flight of new B-24's left for the western Aleutians with the LB-30 showing the way. The "Kiska Blitz" was about to start and it would be hard on the Americans. No sooner did Japanese lookouts sound an alert than their 75mm shells raced skyward to greet the bombers. One shell exploded *inside* a B-24 which had just opened the bomb bay doors. The explosion completely tore the plane apart and damaging two other bombers nearby, all this at 15,000 ft. altitude. In less than half-a-minute the B-24's turned around for home.

Score: One shot down
  Two severely damaged
  Two OK.

The two "good" planes had dropped their bombs but results were undetected.

Back at Umnak, the B-17's were ready to go just as the first flight straggled in. Eareckson changed tactics immediately when he learned of the damage the Japanese had inflicted on precision, high-flying bombers in formation. Each would now go in on his own at low level, wiggle through the valleys between the volcanoes and bomb Japanese positions, hopefully before the enemy knew they were overhead. Eareckson would be the flight leader. The Japanese did not have RADAR.

That flight must have been a show-stopper! The Japanese were

American photo of Kiska Harbor. Marine railway for hauling seaplanes, midget submarines out of water on right. Note dispersed RUFE fighter planes and MAVIS bomber at left. Japanese base considered a permanent installation. Even had fire hydrants.

taken completely by surprise as B-17's stood on wing tips scooting through the valleys. They dropped bombs aimed at two cruisers and three destroyers and missed every one of them! Eareckson was peeved but only for a moment. They'd go back on the morrow at even lower level!

Captain Gehres was also peeved and highly stressed. He really couldn't instigate any battle plans for his Catalinas on his own as his boss, "Fuzzy" Theobald, was still in radio silence out there somewhere – position unknown. Gehres' new fleet of P-boats were amphibians and had RADAR!

Gehres took the bull by the horns, assumed command and radioed Nimitz that the Japanese were at Kiska and he was ready to attack. Nimitz agreed. The tender, U.S.S. *Gillis* was at Atka so the PBY's were flown there. With Nimitz OK to start Navy air offensives at Kiska, Gehres wrote the orders: Attack Kiska with full bomb loads and make a shuttle service of the raids until the Japanese are driven out or there are no more bombs to drop.

There would be no stopping if the weather was bad. But Catalina flying boats were never intended for such assignment and

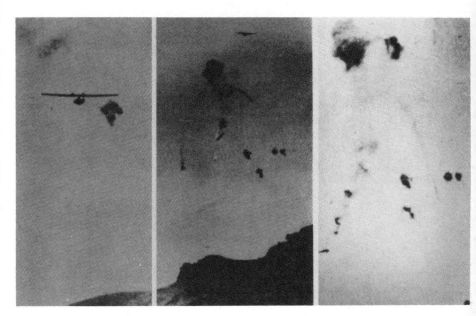

PBY on bombing run over Kiska hit by anti-aircraft fire, explodes.
(Lower) One of many guns on Kiska abandoned by Japanese
when they evacuated the island under cloak of fog.

63

Bombed hanger (top) on Kiska. Entrance to Japanese bomb shelter.

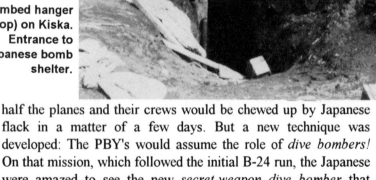

half the planes and their crews would be chewed up by Japanese flack in a matter of a few days. But a new technique was developed: The PBY's would assume the role of *dive bombers!* On that mission, which followed the initial B-24 run, the Japanese were amazed to see the new *secret-weapon dive bomber* that looked some-thing like a PBY that had damaged a destroyer.

Captain Gehres' "Blitz" was giving the Japanese a pasting every hour, day and night, rain or shine! And that wasn't all. Even

Shinto shrine on Kiska

though the B-l7's and B-24's had to fly 1,200 miles round trip from Umnak, these heavies, now bombing at "deck level" with delayed action fuses so the planes could get out before their bombs exploded, managed two round trips a day.

Then the Japanese sent up a surprise: "RUFE" fighter planes. These were Zero's (ZEEKS) with pontoons that had been sent to ·Kiska! (There were already several "MAVIS" huge 4-engine flying boat patrol bombers there.)

The blitz was trying on everybody. American air crews were plainly "pooped." American crews on tender *Gillis* were sleepless from the 24 hour servicing of the P-boats.

Kawanishi 97 "MAVIS" 4-engine long-range (1,000 mile) flying-boat patrol bomber was designed as 20-passenger civil aircraft. Had 103 ft 3 inch wingspan, 84 ft. long. Top speed 190 mph at 8,000 ft. alt. had two 20mm cannons, several 7.7mm machine guns and crew of 10. Six MAVIS were stationed at Kiska of which 5 were shot down.

Village of Atka on Nazan Bay. Photo believed made about 1950.

Chapter 9
Japanese Countermeasures

At Atka village, the lady school teacher had been cooking three meals a day for 50 men, in her home, and turned the school room into an infirmary which she also attended. Gehres' order to continuously bomb Kiska had not run the Japanese off the island but *Gillis* had now run out of bombs.

One of the MAVIS giant flying boats started snoop flights among the islands to locate where the Catalinas were based. The Japanese couldn't imagine there were so many that a continuous stream would be coming from as far as Dutch Harbor. They reasoned there must be a tender hiding somewhere. They photographed *Gillis* at Atka and in reporting the find, code-breaker Joe Rochefort picked up part of the message in Honolulu. He cracked enough of it to get Nimitz to order *Gillis* to scram fast! *Gillis'* skipper, Lt. Commander Norman F. Garton, sent a whaleboat ashore to fetch all the men and to *invite** all the natives and Mrs. Oliver, the teacher, to join the ship as the enemy was coming. Before all had pulled out, the navy burned down the village so it would be useless to the Japanese who indeed promptly showed up.

As the Americans withdrew to Umnak, now their most westerly post, the Japanese "can of worms" was opening in their two "conquered" islands. The supply line just to keep the troops fed and supplied with shells for anti-aircraft guns was long and costly. From Paramushiro, the most northerly base in Japan, it was 800 miles to Kiska and slightly less to Attu. Admiral Yamamoto delegated Aleutian matters to the elderly, and very

*The destroyer *Hulbert*, according to Morison, had been sent from Cold Bay to Atka to support *Gillis* and may have participated in the evacuation of 62 Aleuts. This invitation to evacuate was, in the mid-1980's, grounds for Aleuts to claim they were "relocated" against their will. Their demand for "redress and reparations" was included in Public Law 100-383 (August 10, 1988), the so-called "Japanese Money Bill." The facts surrounding this misunderstood issue are in Baker, *American and Japanese Relocation in World War II; Fact, Fiction & Fallacy.*

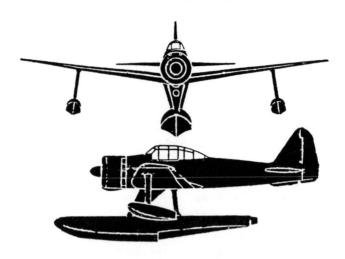

RUFE fighter was float plane modification of famous Zero ZEKE. 39 ft. 5 inch wing-span, 33 ft. 8 inch length. Speed limited to 265 mph at 16,000 ft. alt. due to drag of floats. Range 590 miles.

ly showed up.

As the Americans withdrew to Umnak, now their most westerly post, the Japanese "can of worms" was opening in their two "conquered" islands. The supply line just to keep the troops fed and supplied with shells for anti-aircraft guns was long and costly. From Paramushiro, the most northerly base in Japan, it was 800 miles to Kiska and slightly less to Attu. Admiral Yamamoto delegated Aleutian matters to the elderly, and very Spartan, Admiral Hosogaya.

Both sides moved reinforcements into the foggy Aleutians. As we have seen, Japan shipped in RUFE fighter aircraft to meet the heavy American bombing program over Kiska. (At that time Attu was beyond range of U.S. planes based at Unmak.)

Admiral Yamamoto feared a gigantic American counter attack which he also envisioned not stopping merely at Kiska and Attu, but pushing westward at least to Paramushiro—Japan's front door. The Admiral must have read General Billy Mitchells words about the Aleutians being the jumping off place from which to smash Japan.

Although badly mauled following Midway, Yamamoto transferred aircraft and personnel to carriers *Zuiho* and *Zuikaku* and sent these along with battleships *Kongo* and *Hiei,* cruisers *Tone, Chikuma, Myoko* and *Haguro* and destroyers to Admiral Hosogaya. With this gift of a fleet, Yamamoto sent his blessing and a stout admonition: Find and sink the elusive American fleet.

Yamamoto believed this would be his final chance to put what was left of the U.S. Navy on the bottom of the ocean.

As Theobald had been unable to find the Japanese attack force that had bombed Dutch Harbor twice in two days, Admiral Nimitz, on the heels of his victory at Midway, ordered two American carriers, six cruisers and ten destroyers to the Aleutians to help. Rear Admiral Raymond A. Spruance was in command.

Spruance's carriers were the *Enterprise* and the *Hornet* – the pair that had been part of the Doolittle raid. When about half-way to Alaska, this force was recalled when Nimitz got Gehres' message that the Japanese fleet – at least part of it – was being bombed.

Admiral Kakuta, now with four carriers the *Ryujo, Junyo, Zuikaku* and *Zuiho,* two battleships and four heavy cruisers, had a right to feel pretty proud about his large command. He grouped through the fog for several weeks seeking the American fleet. As time and fuel for his ships were being expended with no contacts, Admiral Yamamoto grew tired of the exercise.

During the first week of July, just as American submarines in the Aleutians were beginning to sink miscellaneous vessels of the Kiska Command, Hosogaya received notice that Imperial Head-quarters was recalling all his carriers and all the cruisers. This left him with a few destroyers, a seaplane tender, three MAVIS flying boat bombers (about twice the size of a PBY) and the squadron of RUFE fighters. With this force, plus some cargo ships, he was supposed to maintain his outposts at Kiska and at Attu and also beat off American attempts to dislodge him. With this severe reduction in his power, the "worms " were squirming out of the can and the Japanese could not contain them.

*   *   *

The summer of 1942 was to be filled with major encounters between Japan and the United States elsewhere in the Pacific Ocean, thus it could appear to some that both governments almost let the western Aleutians "die on the vine." Admiral Nimitz requested his Alaska Commanders, Theobald and Buckner, to give the Japanese a bad time with constant bomb runs – haras-

Consolidated B-24 (LB-30) "LIBERATOR" 4-engine heavy bomber. Wingspan 110 ft. Length 66 ft. 4 inches. Speed 320+ mph. Ceiling 26,500 ft. Range with 8,000 lbs bombs, 1,600 miles. Maximum range 3,200 miles.

sment — as he realized there was insufficient manpower and equipment to expel the Japanese.

Between the American Navy and Air Force, the Japanese couldn't catch their breath. If and when the weather was clear, the B-17's and B-24's did high-level precision bombing then without notice skipped from one target and another as low as 700 feet above the bay. On one such run, Eareckson's pilots dropped homemade incendiaries – rubber bags full of gasoline! These odd tactics included "flying splinters of glass" when cases of empty beer and Coca Cola bottles were dropped shattering on impact. Occasionally bombs hit something important. Other times all they did was keep the Japanese pinned down which was the object.

In Washington, D.C., government spokesmen were "mum" about the Aleutians. *Silence!* It was not until June 21 that the press was told:

> The enemy inflicted minor damage to the Naval Station at Dutch Harbor and the Army post at Fort Mears, but did not seriously impair their military effectiveness. The enemy had occupied the undefended islands of Attu, Kiska and Agattu [about 30 miles from Attu] in the westernmost tip of the Aleutians....

The American people were denied the news because of U.S. Naval censorship although reports had been coming in for days from persons with radios capable of tuning in "Tokyo Rose."

Chapter 10
Submarine Activity – Western Aleutians

Both Japanese and American submarines sortied in the Aleutians. At the on set, Japan had large, fleet, aircraft-carrier submarines on patrols which extended all the way to Puget Sound and the Columbia River.* About this time, Admiral Yamamoto stripped Admiral Hosogaya of the larger elements of the fleet assigned to Aleutian waters, the I-class boats were pulled back and smaller, older, RO submarines sent in. RO boats were of a vintage of the early-to-mid 1920's. They were about equal to the American S-boats assigned to Theobald soon after he arrived at Kodiak but each navy recognized these submarines as serviceable under limited conditions.

Among their major drawbacks of the RO's was their diving depth limitation. They could not go below the exploding depth of modern depth charges. On August 31, *RO-61* would be sunk by U.S.S. *Reid* after the submarine torpedoed and badly damaged seaplane tender U.S.S. *Casco* in the favorite seaplane base, Nazan Bay, Atka Island. The *Reid's* skipper, Commander Harold Pullen, sent a message to skipper Commander Thomas S. Combs on the now beached and burning *Casco*:

GOT SUB THAT GOT YOU. HAVE FIVE PRISONERS FOR PROOF

It was the Americans who first "invaded" Amchitka even though their landing was caused by an accident. *S-27* was scouting Amchitka when, without RADAR, the boat plowed into a rock in 15-foot high surf. As the pig-boat flooded, the crew went

---

*The historic attacks against a British Columbia lighthouse at Estevan Point and on Fort Stevens, a coast artillery post in the vicinity of Astoria, Oregon, and many dozens of other attacks on the American mainland, including the killing of school children in Oregon by a Japanese bomb, is thoroughly covered in *Silent Siege III; Japanese Attacks On North America in World War II, Ships Sunk, Air Raids, Bombs Dropped, Civilians Killed.* (See bibliography)

U.S.S. *S-44* (SS149)

On September 26, 1943, *S-44* (Lt. Cdr. F. E. Brown) left Attu on her 5th war patrol this time to snoop the Northern Kuriles as there was known shipping off Paramushiro.

On October 7th, during a pitch black night, the submarine made RADAR contact with what was interpreted to be a merchantman. The gunners were ordered on deck then the *S-44* began to close on the ship' to deliver a surprise surface attack. Brown opened fire but got his own surprise in the form of a studding salvo from what turned out to be a destroyer.

Brown immediately ordered everyone off the deck and sounded for a crash dive but his submarine did not respond. One of the Japanese shells had smashed his control room. The next shell exploded in the conning tower and a third crashed his hull at the forward battery room.

The order to abandon the vessel was passed and a crewman waved a pillow case as a flag of surrender but the Japanese pressed the attack. Death on the *S-44* seemed to be the main activity for only seven or eight escaped into the sea. Of those just two were fished out by the destroyer. These were Chief Torpedoman Mate E. A. Duva and Radioman 3rd Class W. A. Whitemore. The survivors were landed at Paramushiro then transferred to Naval Interrogation Camp, Ofuna. Later they were forced into labor in copper mines of Ashio until rescued by Americans at the end of the war.

About this time the *S*-boats were taken off active patrols and returned to the U. S. as training vessels. It was the lot of the *S-44* to go down in the last *S*-boat battle in the Pacific War.

ashore on Amchitka to make camp in the abandoned Russian Church at Constantine Harbor. With the food salvaged from *S-27,* the men sustained themselves for a week until spotted by a patrolling PBY that, with other planes, picked up everyone. Nimitz realized the need for modern submarines in the northern waters so as new construction was launched and reached the Pacific, he sent in eight new boats. Among them was *Growler.* On her first war patrol the submarine sneaked into Kiska's harbor then let go three torpedoes: bam...bam....bam...! Destroyer *Arare,* struck amid-ships, sank in minutes. Destroyer *Kasumi* had its bow nearly blown off. *Shiranuhi's* hull was broken in two. Lt. Cdr. oward W. Gilmore rigged for silent running and quietly headed for the open sea between severe depth charge attacks. He arrived at Dutch Harbor safely but with some broken parts.

Triton was patrolling off Attu when her sonar picked up destroyer *Nenohi.* After 10 hours of stalking, Lt. Cdr. Charles C. Kirkpatrick let go of two of his "fish." They shattered the destroyer. It sank quickly in the icy water with all its crew.

Grunion (Lt. Cdr. Mannert L. Abele) on her first war patrol, went after a par of sub-chasers (*SC-25* and *SC-27*) and sank both then tried for a 3rd near Kiska. Damaged it. A little later, still near Kiska, *Grunion* radioed there was heavy enemy ship traffic near Kiska. On July 30, 1942, she reported but that was the last ever heard from *Grunion.* Post-war evaluations by Japanese and American study teams were unable to determine why this new submarine was lost or exactly where it happened.

On July 14, Japanese sub *I-7* was also prowling and sighted a transport, U.S.A.T. *Arcata,* in Unimak Pass. Surfacing, *I-7s* gunners poured 5.5-inch shells into the ship, causing the *Arcata* to sink. This action took a lot of shells before the ship sank.

During this period, while Admiral Hosogaya had his large force, he made up a convoy for Kiska and doubled the numbers of troops on the island.

Earlier we pointed out that Buckner and Theobald were not good company for each other. The situation did not improve with time. If anything, it deteriorated. Further, Buckner didn't particularly care for Air Force General Wm. O. Butler. And Butler didn't think very kindly toward his Bomber Command head man,

S.S. *Arcata* was sunk in Unimak Pass by shelling from Japanese submarine *I-7*'s deck gun.

Colonel Eareckson. Then there was Navy Captain Leslie Gehres who was running his private PBY war at Kiska.

Gehres had never checked out in P-boats but he had a high-intensity track record in airplanes. He had been a carrier pilot and a member of the Navy's aerobatic team in the National Air Races. He was a hot-shot and he knew it. He found himself to be in Chester Nimitz's "craw" now and then and Nimitz had to warn Gehres to watch his free-wheeling steps. Finally, Nimitz placed Gehres' PBY Wing under Butler of the 11th Air Force. Butler liked having more airplanes to shuttle around but navy man Gehres, very peeved, did not cotton to taking his orders from Air Force's Butler; but there was nothing he could do about it.

All this interservice in-fighting was kept from the public – *silence* – by War and Navy Department spokesmen. It seems remarkable that anything battle-wise against the Japanese was accomplished with this general disagreement in the upper command. General Butler wanted Gehres to stop his runs over Kiska but Gehres continued anyway in the face of the recently arrived RUFE fighters where the waddling P-boats were like sitting ducks. Gehres, in about six weeks, lost four PBY's and half their crews. Theobald didn't like this but left the matter alone as Gehres was, technically, under Butler's thumb at this time. But at Pearl Harbor, the big boss, Admiral Nimitz, began to look closely at the command structure in the Aleutians.

Chapter 11
Eareckson: The One-Man Air Force

Colonel William O. Eareckson, Bomber Command, was out to kill Japanese and if he had the equipment and the supply backup, he was ready to blast them first off Kiska then Attu. But there was another limitation: he was not the supreme commander in the Aleutians and he was sometimes reminded of this. Never-the-less, he recognized the need to do a job so without any fanfare he set about it. His ideas for bombing Kiska were totally different from how the crews had been taught in flight school for, he reasoned, the target – Kiska – was not a flat bombing range in the desert of southern California.

The Japanese commander at Kiska was getting tired of the continuous bombing by the Catalinas and, as we have seen, he set out with his MAVIS's to get the tender. We are reminded that all of the early PBY's were pure seaplanes and had to have a tender or a naval base with mooring buoys at which to tie up. When replacement planes came to the Aleutians, these were the amphibian models (PBY5A), Catalina's with wheels. Imperial Japanese Navy Captain Sukemitsu Ito truly tried to locate the tenders. When *Casco* had been damaged at Nazan Bay, he thought that would end his troubles. But the U.S. Navy moved in tender, *Gillis* (Cdr. Norman F. Garton*)*, in short order.

On August 3, Ito led his three MAVIS bombers to Kuluk Bay, Adak, where *Gillis* was stationed. He planned on pounding *Gillis* into floating trash. An earlier attempt had been disappointing to the Japanese because *Gillis* and destroyer *Kane* dodged all the bombs these flying boats were dropping.

Eareckson knew the MAVIS's would be back so he set a trap.

> Fact: P-38's didn't have RADAR so they could not find targets in the overcast.
> Fact: The B-17's had RADAR.

Eareckson reversed the roles of fighters leading bombers, and sent the bombers out to spot for the incoming Japanese.

Sure enough! One of the Fortress's RADAR operators tapped out a coded message to Eareckson that the three Japanese flying boats were lumbering in. The position was quickly relayed to the waiting P-38's that immediately peeled off through the overcast pouring machine gun and 20mm cannon fire at the bombers.

The Japanese crews were taken by complete surprise. It was all Captain Ito could do to get his lumbering Kawanishi 97 (MAVIS) into a cloud. The P-38's shot down the other two. Of Ito's original squadron of 6 MAVIS's, he had only one left. He had been outsmarted so he took his remaining flying boat back to Japan. This sortie was the first victory for P-38 "Lightning" fighters in World War II.

Eareckson was a man with a mission: harass the Japanese! He sent out a daily "weather" flight to be usually told "no flying today – socked in" but often his planes went anyway. The aerial photos of Kiska revealed where every anti-aircraft position was located and Eareckson warned his pilots about them. The low-altitude side-slipping flights continued with the old-timer crews while new units flew the "text-book" high altitude precision ranges, dropping bombs through clouds hopefully hitting the right island.

Obviously, the distance from McChord Field or McClellan Field (Air Depots) in Washington and California respectively, was too far to have to wait for parts. When an airplane cracked up – and bad landings in bad weather became common – the planes, if they could not be repaired, were broken up for parts. It is doubtful that any of Eareckson's original B-17's or B-24's had very many original parts remaining in them. Although the engineering officers continued to declare many of Bomber Command's planes "unfit to fly," Eareckson's ground crews made up of skilled repairmen – mostly enlisted men – kept the planes flyable. The weather was more of an enemy than the Japanese.

The B-17, "Old 70" had been in the air every day, frequently on the weather run as she had longer range being lighter weight. But the weather itself caught the plane on a return from Kiska, full of bullet holes as usual, and the B-17 crashed into a mountain. All those holes were from the RUFE fighters which now rose to greet every bombing mission. Even so, the many machine guns on the B-1 7's knocked RUFE out of the air, but RUFE got hits too shooting down B-1 7s and B-24s.

Eareckson, as commander of the Bomber unit, and a Colonel, could have stayed in the Operations shack and directed his planes by radio and with ground briefings. But he was a pilot and he loved to be in the air. He frequently led his bombers on the new tactics he had developed to show them how to do it.

On July 24, the command was brought together for the presentation of the Distinguished Service Cross to Eareckson. In fact, it was the first mass military formation on Umnak. A portion of the citation for bravery reads:

INSTEAD OF REMAINING IN COMPARATIVE SAFETY AT HIS HEADQUARTERS, HE REPEATEDLY TOOK TO THE AIR TO DIRECT PERSONAL ATTACKS AGAINST THE ENEMY, AND PERSONALLY FILLED GAPS ON NUMEROUS FLIGHTS BY ACTING IN EVERY CAPACITY FROM FIRST PILOT TO GUNNER...

I was a crew chief on B-17's and B-24's with 36th Bomb Sqdn and the Japs on Kiska and Attu were our targets.. We lost a lot of men and aircraft mostly to bad, bad weather . We were a rough and tumble gang of soldiers and gentlemen. Col. Eareckson, our C.O., wanted only men that would out-think, out fight, out gamble, out do in all ventures. They had to prove their worth as frightening as it was.   —Michael M. Rudy. USAF-ret.
New Glarus, Wisconsin

I was on Adak where we ran a secret radio station and direction finder there to spot enemy planes if they came around.
—Dave King, USN (ret) Dallas, Texas

Chapter 12
First American Naval Sorties at Kiska

Admiral Nimitz had listened to about enough from Admiral Theobald. Nimitz's Aleutian commander was continuing to complain of not enough ships and there was his lengthy list of "problems" with Buckner and with the Air Force. Nimitz was aware the bombers had been on the job plastering Kiska daily while Theobald was either "churning water" on *Nashville* somewhere at sea, under radio silence, or sitting in his office at Kodiak. Nimitz plainly wanted Theobald to "do something." He provided some extra ships so now it was up to Theobald.

This time Theobald carried his flag to U.S.S. *Indianapolis* (Captain Morton L. Deyo) a heavy cruiser, and on July 19th, Theobald ordered his entire "fleet" to head for Kiska.

Cruisers	Destroyers	Mine sweepers
Indianapolis❖	Case	Lamberton+
Louisville	Reid	Elloitt
Honolulu	Gridley	Long+
Nashville	McCall	Chandler+
St. Louis	Monaghan+	
		Auxiliary
		Guadalupe (tanker)

❖ Flag ship   +Damaged during the mission

The tanker topped off all the ships' fuel tanks when the flotilla neared its objective. Theobald was pleased to be on the move. But he fidgeted a lot because the fog seemed unusually thick. Finally, he postponed the planned action and retired the ships away from Kiska. On his return a few days later, the soup – fog – "cream-thick fog" as Morison wrote it, was again too much for Theobald so he again turned the fleet away.

Every ship in formation must move as a unit to avoid accidents. All should have gone well, even in a soupy fog for the 90°

turn ordered to affect the retirement. Obviously, because of what happened, some ships were not where they should have been. The two mine sweepers crunched together and a third was rammed by destroyer *Monaghan*.

Alas! Admiral Theobald gave up never having fired a shot at the Japanese. He took his fleet all the way back to Kodiak.

Quietly on August 3, Admiral Nimitz took Theobald's ten undamaged ships away from him and ordered Rear Admiral William W. "Poco" Smith to get back out to Kiska. "Fuzzy" Theobald found himself consigned to his desk at Kodiak.

Admiral Theobald was a brilliant navy career man and had finished 9th in the class of 1907 at Annapolis. He had successful Quietly on August 3, Admiral Nimitz took Theobald's ten undamaged ships away from him and ordered Rear Admiral William W. "Poco" Smith to get back out to Kiska. "Fuzzy" Theobald found himself consigned to his desk at Kodiak.

Admiral Theobald was a brilliant navy career man and had finished 9th in the class of 1907 at Annapolis. He had successful with earlier commands and should have been right for this job. But he felt he had been marooned by the Navy in a place he utterly hated: the Aleutians. After all the frustrations in the north he was sick of "the Navy, the Air Force, the Army (particularly General Buckner), the Sea Bees, *the weather...*" and the seagulls!

Exercising considerably more daring, "Poco" Smith went back to Kiska (without the damaged ships) but this time with a flock of PBYs as "escort" After some anxious moments in the fog, the weather cleared long enough for some of the men to actually see their objective. But, using old tactics, the Admiral had his force shooting cannons at between *eight and eleven miles from the target!* Even so, the Japanese spent their time in their caves watching for and dodging incoming shells. One barracks was blown up. Several landing barges were smashed. A MAVIS was sunk at mooring. *Kano Maru*, a freighter already internally troubled earlier by a *Grunion* torpedo, caught fire and was sunk by PBYs the next day.

Probably because the American attackers were so far away and couldn't really see what they were shooting at, five ships and a flock of midget subs were missed. No one said how many, if

79

any, casualties had been inflicted on the Japanese.

American losses? The cruisers had launched Kingfisher (OS2U) observation seaplanes to spot results of the big guns but these little pigeons had been swooped upon by RUFE fighters like hawks. One spotter was lost but the others scrambled for the fog bank. One RUFE, acting as a spotter, roared around at 300 miles per hour, too fast for the anti-aircraft on the ships to catch him. A shore battery opened up and landed near-misses. Destroyer *Case* was severely mauled by a RUFE. In half an hour, "Poco" radioed a cease fire. One of the little pigeons had 167 bullet holes including one in the pilot's foot.

-Japanese Names-

Kiska: Narukami-shima
Attu: Atsuta-shima
Adak: Komagata-shima

Submarine *Tuna* (SS-203) did two war patrols in Japanese home waters then was assigned to the Aleutians in July 1942. Her third patrol searched for Japanese targets of opportunity but its only contact was with an *I*-class submarine on August 9. Due to heavy weather, *Tuna's* prey escaped in the fog. *Tuna* then transported a colonel and six enlisted men from Dutch Harbor to Kuluck Bay between Aug 25 and 27. *Tuna* was next sent to Pearl Harbor for overhaul. She then patrolled in Empire and South Pacific waters completing 13 war patrols with a good account in sinkings, shellings and other hazardous duty.   —The Editor

We managed to get a small Post Exchange opened for the anti-aircraft artillery boys on St. Paul Island. By coded radio message by way of Anchorage we ordered a large case of candy bars from a wholesaler in Seattle. Transportation not being all that good we had to wait. And we waited. After what seemed a lifetime, a box came at last. With eagerness we tore it open but we were dumbfounded. We got a gross of condoms instead of a gross of candy bars and there was not a woman around for over 1,000 miles.   —Turnley Addams. DEML
Miami Florida

Chapter 13
Adak and Amchitka

Another sputtering between Theobald and Butler – General Buckner stayed away – had to do with the next move to the west. Butler wanted to plant an airfield on Tanaga. It was fairly flat. Theobald wanted Adak because Adak had a harbor even though the island was not flat.

The order to occupy Adak gave the logisticians only one week to prepare.

Brig. General Eugene M. Landrum, a competent officer who was familiar with the Aleutians and its unique challenges, was detailed to command the landing. Rear Admiral John W. Reeves would handle the Navy's end.

The plan: Land 4,000 men on Adak, which was just 250 miles from Kiska, on a single night. There was no current intelligence on whether there were any Japanese there so General Buckner brought in his commandos, the Alaska Scouts. The Scouts would go in early. If the enemy was there, the Scouts were to eradicate them. Submarines *Tuna* and *Triton,* with the Scouts aboard, slipped through the water and put them ashore on August 28th. It was just a few hours later when an "all clear" signal, in cloth strips, was set out for the patrolling PBY to spot.

General Buckner had a superb construction chief in mind whenever there was a airport to be built. He called in Colonel Benjamin B. Talley. He had been Buckner's chief engineer on the Umnak and Cold Bay landing fields. Talley would have gone to Adak in a Catalina on D-Day except the weather was fierce and the P-boat could not set down. So the PBY dropped into Nazan Bay and moored to the buoy near tender *Casco*. One will recall this was the day when, as destroyer *Reid* left to haul Talley and others to Adak, *RO-61* suddenly came to life from the bay's bottom and put a torpedo into *Casco*. This forced the tender's

Admiral James S. Russell identified the photograph on page 82 in these words:

ADAK: This is a picture of the diversion of the stream running down from Mt. Moffat behind a bulldozed dike and the flying field. The airport is on the bed of what had been the bottom of the lagoon. A tide gate that was opened at low tide then closed at high tide, drained the flat. We had a flying field in operation in just ten days after General Eugene Landrum's troops made an unopposed landing here. The tide gate and Sweeper Cove is off the picture to the right.

Airplanes are visible on the air strip made of 4,000 feet of Marsden steel linked mat. Another 4,000 feet of mat was lost when the lighter carrying it capsized in a storm. But we found we did not need the mat because the hard-packed black, volcanic sand of the lagoon's bottom made a good air field.

(Opposite page) Adak air strip project required drainage and landfill. The first strip was steel. A permanent concrete runway was built later nearby.

skipper to set immediate course for the beach where he parked his ship to keep it from sinking. The *Reid* was detailed as standby. Col. Talley would have to find other transportation to Adak.

On Adak, Buckner's 4th Infantry Regiment managed to get to the beaches in the midst of that fierce storm, the storm keeping Japanese and American spotter planes on the ground some distance away. The crashing breakers the landing troops had to get through, then trying to hold on to slippery rocks, at the same time hauling in equipment, was no vacation day at the beach. The work was just plain tough. Some landing barges were lost cargoes and all, but the "invasion" of unoccupied Adak was completed more-or-less as planned.

Every landing must have a "straw-boss" on the beach directing traffic. This task went to Navy Commander Carl "Squeaky" Anderson. He had been Captain-of-the-Port at Dutch Harbor. "Squeeky's" job was to organize all material as it hit the beach as well as to direct traffic of men as they landed. In fact, he was a routing clerk, stevedore pusher and traffic cop rolled into one.

Elements of the 897th Aviation Engineers, the outfit that built airfields, landed and were soon in with Col. Talley in huddles about where to plant their runways. It would be just ten days later when Colonel Eareckson landed the first airplane at the new field even if it was just hard-packed sand. In a few more days the shipment of steel matting for the runway arrived. It was laid down in a single night.

With the completion of the strip, long distance flights to Kiska were over. Now the run was a mere 240 miles. It was September 13 and winter was moving in as Lt. Commander Jim Russell, who still commanded the PBY Patrol Squadron 42, landed. His amphibian Catalinas would also use the Adak strip.

The next day a maximum effort was launched with Eareckson in the lead plane. There were Airacobras (P-39s), 14 of them into action for the first time. There were 14 P-38s and 12 B-24s. The heavy bombers dumped explosives and got results:

> More than 200 enemy casualties
> Sank two ships
> Broke three midget submarines in their pens
> Set three ships afire
> Collapsed several anti-aircraft batteries.
> A MAVIS and seven RUFE's were wiped out at
>   their moorings.

Five of the Japanese pontoon fighters got into the air but the Airacobras shot them all down. In the melee two P-38's collided, crashed, took their pilots with them.

*　　　*　　　*

Amchitka is a fairly large island, compared to most of the others in the outer chain, and is about 50 miles from Kiska. The Japanese had been thinking of landing some troops there in their own checker board plans. First, they evacuated Agattu's tent camp and moved those troops to Kiska. So far, the only American planes to bomb Attu had been PBY's from tenders as the trip to Attu and back from Umnak was too far for land planes.

With the Japanese on Attu spending their time dodging American bombs, eating groceries and trying to keep warm, Admiral Hosogaya, realizing the Americans lacked strength to push any substantial attack there, took his men to Kiska and abandoned Attu to the "williwaws."

The Battle of Guadalcanal was occupying Admiral Yamamoto's attention and Hosogaya was left with what was becoming his *Aleutian headache*. There was no chance, with most of his ships recalled by Yamamoto, for him to set up a base on Amchitka. To his chagrin, Hosogaya lost any potential offensive action he would otherwise have because he was forced to use his attack-submarines to keep the Aleutian garrisons provisioned with food and ammunition.

Admiral Theobald, a keen strategist, was the one who pushed for the American occupation of Amchitka. He realized if the Japanese got there first, Adak would be in trouble. The Army opposed moving to Amchitka but the joint Chiefs in Washington thought Amchitka looked good so gave the go-ahead.

Theobald would not be on hand to see the occupation of Amchitka for when any branch of the service wants to "make things happen" it brings in men who will do the job without quibbling. On January 4th, 1943, Rear Admiral Thomas C. Kinkaid arrived to relieve Theobald. The decision to remove Theobald was made by Admiral Nimitz only three days earlier.

Kinkaid was an opposite to the always pessimistic, ultra-conservative and always bitter "Fuzzy" Theobald. Kinkaid was a possibility thinker; one who made quick assertive decisions. He was tenacious. He had been in more sea battles than any other Admiral and would "go for broke" when he thought he was on the right track. Besides, he was friendly.

With Kinkaid's arrival another exchange was made. "Poco" Smith was relieved and the strike force of cruisers and destroyers was given to Rear Admiral Charles H. McMorris.

As for the United States Navy in the Aleutians, the Theobald treading-water-period was over.

Eight days later, Brig. General Lloyd E. Jones landed an Army force of 2,100 men on unoccupied Amchitka and dug in to protect themselves from a blizzard.

Colonel Talley was called to move in his engineers to build an air field. A man of action, he was not one to sit around. He had an air strip ready for a squadron of P-40s in fourteen days! While the

Rear Admiral Thomas C. Kinkaid relieved Admiral Theobald on January 14, 1943.

work was in progress, Japanese RUFE fighters, now with bombs attached, made repeated trips to hinder the work. The Japanese had so few planes left at Kiska that the bombing "squadron" was sometimes only two planes. On some days just a single airplane would appear, drop its three bombs then scoot for safety.

Then suddenly, six RUFES appeared. The Japanese had been reinforced! The distance from Kiska was so short that the observers on Amchitka could report when the Japanese planes took off, thus Amchitka was ready for their arrival with P-40's led by Major Jack Chennault. By February 18th, there were no more Japanese air raids, as the RUFES were being shot down regularly. In time P-38, B-25 and B-26 medium bombers were based at Amchitka and sometimes carried out hourly raids on Kiska.

Gehres brought tender *Avocet* into Constantine Harbor from which PBY's now operated. When the runway was extended, the B-24 s and B-17s came in. But Eareckson didn't bring in the first plane this time. He had been sent to the States on special "Buckner business."

With the U.S. now breathing down the Japanese neck such a few miles away, the contents of Admiral Hosogaya's "can of worms" had all squirmed out. The Japanese would have to immediately make a determined stand in the Aleutians or they would have to get out.

On February 5th, Hosogaya got his answer from Imperial Headquarters:

HOLD AT ALL COSTS. PREPARE FOR WAR

Hosogaya had earlier (October 29) put troops back on Attu

with instructions to build an airfield. He wanted a landing field at Kiska too, but had to give it up. The land was too full of rocks, big ones, to move without heavy construction equipment which he did not have and could not get from Japan. On Attu, there was some light equipment but the major airfield building tools were little more than picks, hand shovels and push carts.

Hosogaya had assembled a large force in Paramushiro under Colonel Hiroshi Yanekawa. Together they planned on occupying Shemya as well as going back to Attu. But off Shemya, in the act of preparing to send his troops ashore, an urgent message was received warning of probable trouble from the U.S. Navy which the Japanese believed to be in the vicinity. Hosogaya canceled the landing and hauled out to sea.

The American code breakers at Hawaii had been listening. Intercepting the Japanese "traffic" concerned with the Shemya operations, messages from Rochefort to Theobald had been misinterpreted by the Japanese listeners who "thought" the U.S. was sending a fleet in the direction of the western Aleutians.

With American planes now at Adak, Attu became within reach. On one "trip" American planes found a flight of Zero's on the half-ready airstrip at Attu. The U.S. finished them off and sank a ship in Holtz Bay on the same outing.

High noon view from Kiska.

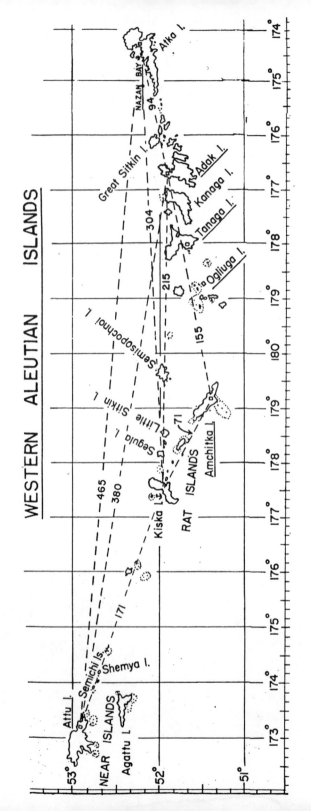

Chapter 14
Kinkaid's Attu Caper

With the major disagreements at the command level apparently settled with the transfer of Admiral Theobald out of the Aleutians, plus the fact that Kinkaid wanted to fight Japanese with aggressive actions, the new naval commander ordered air strikes at Attu. He also prepared his cruiser-destroyer task force for action there. And a rare occurrence in the weather was noted: *visibility unlimited!* It was February 18, 1943.

Cruisers *Richmond* and *Indianapolis* and the four destroyers approached Attu in column. When about five miles off shore, the ships' guns opened up. The column executed reverse course (180°), cranked the gun turrets from starboard to port and raked the island again. There was no return fire as the Japanese apparently had no artillery or for their own reasons decided not to use it. In fact, no movement on the island was noted. The Japanese were dug in. A couple of hours later the American force stopped shooting and put out to sea.

Post-war damage evaluation revealed 23 had been killed and one wounded. One building had been flattened. But the naval bombardment caused a greal deal of nervousness among the Japanese for only four days earlier there had been an air strike during which a direct hit on a bomb shelter had killed fourteen.

Admiral Hosogaya was moving reinforcements and ammunition into the islands at this time. A lookout on *Indianapolis* reported a ship on the horizon. This turned out to be *Akagane Maru*, a 3,100-ton freighter full of ammunition. The cruiser challenged for identification and was preparing to give battle when the clicking of Morse code in the radio shack apparently indicated an answer was coming. But it was katakana-Morse (recognizable but not readable by anyone on the American ships) so the cruiser

Admiral Thomas C. Kinkaid (left) discusses strategy ashore. He had relieved Admiral Theobald and immediately set out to bombard Kiska.

started shooting at 6,700 yards. On the third 8-inch salvo, the freighter erupted in flaming explosions. Amercian destroyers were ordered to move in to sink the ship.

Two other merchant men, not discovered by the Americans, left the area with their cargoes intact and apparently returned to Paramushiro.

Recalling that Washington, D.C. wanted the Japanese off United States soil, and recognizing that the major installation was at Kiska, general conversations as well as planning were aimed at Kiska. Admiral Kinkaid observed, after his sortie to Attu, that Attu should be easier to conquer due to the apparent lack of heavy guns and no more aircraft stationed there. Admiral Chester Nimitz's consultations with the joint Chiefs of Staff concluded that available manpower, as well as equipment for a major move against Kiska, was not yet in the cards. But a liberation of Attu was approved for early May.

On Attu and on Kiska, the pick-and-shovel-carrying troops were doing everything possible to build an airstrip. And every time the U.S. bombers visited – sometimes several times a day – the radios crackled in Imperial Headquarters complaining that the work had to be done all over because of bomb craters. Wouldn't the High Command please bring in some heavy equipment?

Chapter 15
Battle of Komondorski Islands

Every time Japanese radios crackled katakana, Rochefort and his staff at Pearl were listening and writing it down. Their interest was routine when they cracked messages asking for heavy equipment; the complaints of having to rebuild an unfinished air strip due to American bombing, and other ho-hum traffic. But when they picked up a message that indicated Hosogaya would escort a convoy to the Aleutians, leaving Paramushiro on March 22, they sat straight up in their chairs.

Rochefort, who had direct access to Nimitz without having to go through "channels," told Nimetz what was brewing. Nimitz quickly code-messaged Kinkaid in Kodiak. Kinkaid radioed Admiral McMorris who was at sea west of Attu that the convoy was heading his way. McMorris said he would watch for it and he'd be ready.

The two forces at sea were:

United States Ships

Cruisers:	*Salt Lake City* (heavy) (1929) guns:10, 8-inch; 8, 5-inch#
	Richmond (light) (1923) guns: 10, 6-inch; 8, 3-inch*#
Destroyers:	*Bailey* (1942) guns: 4, 5-inch*
	Coghlan (1942) guns: 4, 5-inch*
	Dale (1935) guns: 4, 5-inch*
	Monaghan (1935) guns: 4, 5-inch*

Imperial Japanese Ships

Cruisers:	Maya (heavy) (1932) guns: 10, 8-inch; 4, 4.7-inch #
	Nachi (heavy) (1928) guns:10, 7.9-inch; 6, 4.7-inch*#
	Abukuma (light) (1925)guns: 7, 5.5-inch; 2, 13-pounder*#
	Tama (light) (1921) guns: 7, 5.5-inch; 2, 13-pounder*
Destroyers:	*Hatsuchimo* (1934) guns: 5, 5-inch *
	Ikazuchi (1932) guns: 6, 5-inch; *
	Inazuma (1932) guns: 6, 5-inch;
	Wakaba (1934) guns: 5, 5-inch *
Merchantmen:	*Asaka Maru*
	Sakito Maru
Freighter	*Sanho Maru*

---

* Torpedoes   # Observation aircraft   Sources: American: *see* Morison. Japanese: *see* Watts & Gordon

In weight and firepower, the Japanese Northern Force was about twice as powerful as the American battle group.*

McMorris' objective was to sink the transports and to inflict damage on the fighting ships as best he could. He realized he was out-gunned and both his cruisers were slower than the Japanese cruisers. At 8:38 a.m., one of the Japanese ships fired on *Richmond* from 2,000 yards and missed. This was just as *Richmond* turned to take a columnar position behind *Salt Lake City*. At 8:42, *Salt Lake City* ("Old Swayback") answered the challenge and opened the battle with a salvo of 8-inch shells from forward turret aimed at *Nachi*.

In classic tradition for the start of a running sea battle, Admiral McMorris passed a general order:

> Tie down everything or throw it overboard
> Release prisoners from the brig
> Make sandwiches
> Put on the coffee pot

Admiral McMorris had his flag in *Richmond*. Hosogaya, in *Nachi*, decided to send his shells in the direction of *Salt Lake City* the largest ship in his opposition. He notified his other cruisers of his intention.

Salt Lake City's fourth salvo caught *Nachi* at the base of the bridge but firemen quickly brought the blaze under control. During this activity, the generator supplying power to the forward part of *Nachi* quit. This put the forward turret out of action.

Hosogaya had messaged the transport skippers to stay on their course for Attu and to stay out of the action. With a feeling that the American commandant would run after the transports, he ordered *Nachi* to close on *Salt Lake City* between the American cruiser and the transports. In a running battle that saw tight turns at maximum speeds, shots were exchanged. *Nachi* fired eight torpedoes at *Salt Lake City*. All missed. Captain Bertram Rodgers continued to put the 585-feet long heavy cruiser through grueling maneuvers by running at 25 of its 32.5-knots. *Richmond*, 555-feet long, maximum speed 35 knots, following as closely as

*An older rule-of-thumb to determine, at a glance, the difference between heavy and light cruisers was the heavies mounted 8-inch guns and the light cruisers were armed with 5-inch guns. There were, however, numerous exceptions. As new construction during WW-II came off the ways, specifications changed.

Japanese cruiser *Abukuma* in Aleutians. Vessel was 500 ft. long of 5,170 tons identifiable by its 3 stacks and high, thick bridge. To thwart identification, Japanese later painted center stack white so it was hard to see on foggy days.

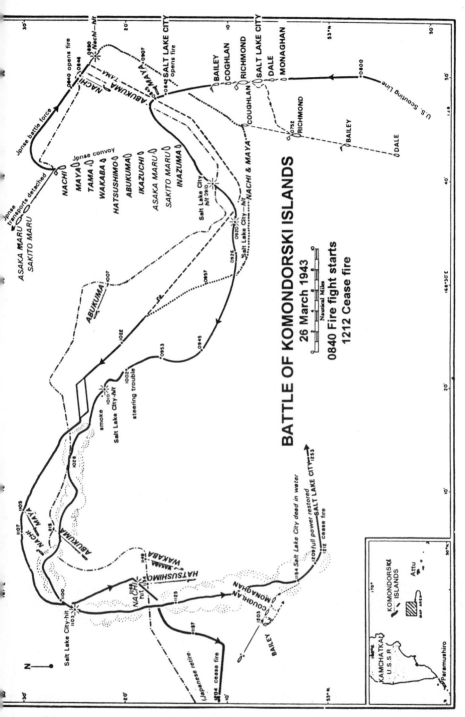

BATTLE OF KOMONDORSKI ISLANDS
26 March 1943
0840 Fire fight starts
1212 Cease fire

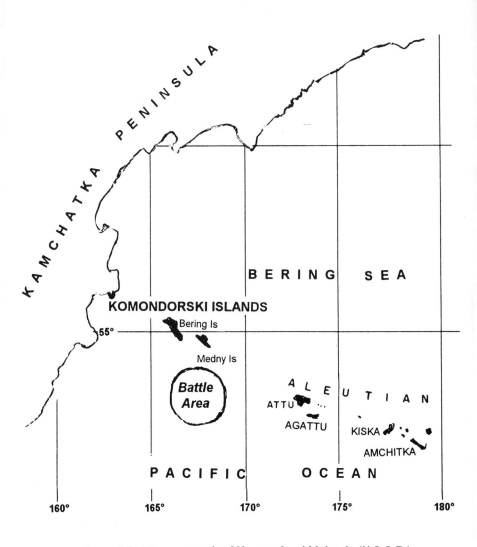

Area of Battle was south of Komondorski Islands (U.S.S.R.)
about halfway between Attu and Kamchatka Peninsula.

conditions permitted.

But the Japanese cruisers were doing at least 30 knots and closing. *Nachi* was squarely hit three-in-a-row against the main mast and bridge. In a few minutes, an 8-inch shell burst on the bridge killing several officers but missed the Admiral.

Salt Lake City wasn't hit until 9:10 when a shell exploded amidships-starboard, killing two men. Damage: light. *Maya* had also been shooting. *Richmond's* 6-inch guns were not often in range so fired infrequently.

Although both commanders had radioed their bases for air strikes, none came. Japanese response: no planes available. American response: armed with bombs for Kiska. Would have to rearm with armor-piercing bombs. There would be a delay. The situation became unique.

> This was a ship-to-ship battle without air support and would be the only such battle of the Pacific War.

U.S.S. *Coghlan* got in a shot which exploded over *Nachi's* troublesome forward turret killing everyone in it.

IJN *Nachi*

Heavy cruiser U.S.S. *Salt Lake City,* **damaged and dead-in-the-water during Battle of Komondorski Islands. Japanese abandoned the battle – went home.**

Salt Lake City took a shell through her main deck which went all the way to an engine room at the bottom. Water poured in and the cruiser slowed. Destroyers were sent to "make smoke" to hide the sight from Admiral Hosogaya, but the damaged American cruiser was seen from time to time as it slipped out of the smoke screen. At two minutes after 10 o'clock, the steering gear hydraulics on this American heavy cruiser went out due to the continued shocks from the big guns. Steer a cruiser by hand?

The *Salt Lake City* was feeling ill by this time as over 200 shells had exploded either as near-misses or on her. She had slowed and *Nachi* and *Maya* were closing. The Japanese kept shooting. About an hour later, *Salt Lake City* was hit below the waterline which flooded the gyros and split fuel tanks. The old lady took a 5° list to port. At one point, engineers turned a wrong valve which rushed icy sea water into the fuel line then into the engines. The ship lost headway. In shock at this incident, Captain Rodgers hoisted signal flags: *Speed zero,* but according to Morison, he had to clear-language radio McMorris because incoming shots from the Japanese shot up his signals flags!

At this point, had the various Japanese ships been alert to the situation, and had Admiral Hosogaya pressed his commanders for more information, the Admiral probably could have determined that *Salt Lake City* was now a sitting duck. She was dead in the water and could be picked off easily. But an extra-ordinary cir-

Line of Japanese cruisers in Aleutian waters.

cumstance occurred.

Salt Lake City ran out of armor-piercing shells which had been marked with blue dye for the spotters so switched to undyed high-explosive shells.

When Hosogaya saw the white plumes instead of blue, he panicked. He was of the opinion that he was being bombed by aircraft. (By this time *Salt Lake City* had shot about 85 percent of her shells.) *Nachi's* crew, truly believing they were being bombed, started shooting anti-aircraft guns into the high clouds hoping to hit something which, of course was not there.

In the meantime, on hearing Rodgers voice-radio, McMorris ordered *Richmond* and destroyer *Dale* to prepare to take off the crew from the seemingly badly damaged *Salt Lake City* He also radioed Kinkaid at Kodiak of the situation and added that the destroyers were passing the attack.

A salvo from the Japanese caught *Bailey* and cut off all electricity but even so, *Bailey* launched a spread of torpedoes before losing headway. When *Coghlan* and *Monaghan* were about 9,000 yards off *Nachi,* all the Japanese ships suddenly wheeled in a tight starboard (westward) turn and, hulls down, quit the battle!

Salt Lake City's engineers cleaned out the fuel line, got the engines going and within four minutes the heavy cruiser was making headway. But the shooting was over.

American casualties were: 7 dead (2 in the cruiser and 5 in *Bailey);* 7 men were in ships' hospitals and there were 13 walking wounded. The water temperature was 28° F and air temperature about 34" F. Skipper Rodgers ordered a shot of "medicinal alcohol" for all hands.

The shell which had put out Bailey's electrical works also took out the galley. For the homeward trip, the crew ate canned ham, soda crackers and drank apple juice.

For the Japanese, there were 14 dead, 27 hurt, all but one on *Nachi.*

American Admiral Kinkaid messaged:

WELL DONE

From the Japanese side, the High Command of the Imperial Navy fired Admiral Hosogaya for failing to sink *Salt Lake City* when he had the chance.

Fletcher Sanders on the Cruiser *Richmond*

I have a vivid memory of the bitter cold and the wind off the ice in the Bering Sea. We wore foul-weather gear with face mask and goggles and we were still very uncomfortable. I was a torpedoman and manned the catapults to fire and retrieve the two scout planes we carried. On March 26 we picked up Jap ships on RADAR. The Japs fired on our starboard bow as we were getting our st'b'd plane ready to launch but that was secured just as another salvo straddled our *Richmond.* It was so close I got soaked with the big splash.

The destroyer *Bailey* and another DD made a most daring torpedo run against the Japs in open daylight at great risk. Both DD's were hit especially *Bailey.* Our *Salt Lake City* was also hit quite bad and went dead in the water a sitting duck for the Japs. I was on the *Richmond* from Nov. 1940 until spring '44. She holds a soft spot in my heart all these years. *Richmond* was a lucky ship.

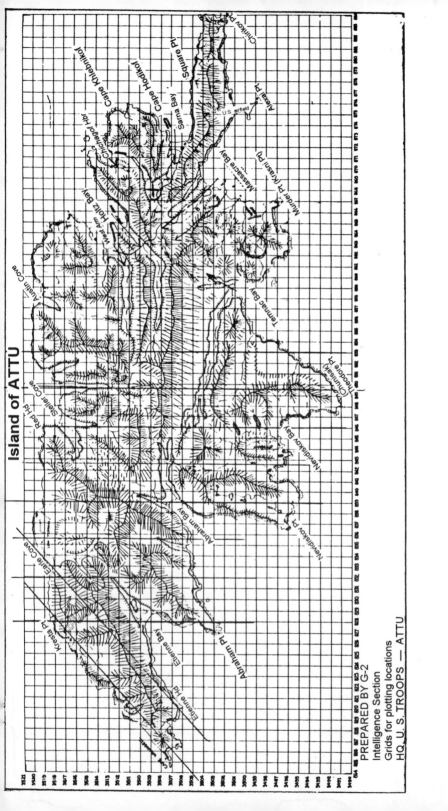

Island of ATTU

PREPARED BY G-2
Intelligence Section
Grids for plotting locations
HQ. U. S. TROOPS — ATTU

Chapter 16
Attu Liberated

Although the 7th Infantry Division invaded Kwajalein, Leyte and Okinawa, it cut its battle teeth at Attu. And Attu was a rude beginning.

When the retaking of the western Aleutians was first contemplated, Kiska was the target but the joint Chiefs of Staff put Kiska aside in favor of Attu. The reasons were simple enough. Kiska, well fortified, manned by thousands of troops, would require a major expedition. Attu, on the other hand, had almost no fortifications and aerial photographs appeared to show minimal personnel.

With the Battle of the Komondorskis behind them and the probability that reinforcements from Paramushiro would never be sent, it seemed that Attu would be the better target. In addition, with Attu in American hands, it would be relatively easy to put airports on Attu and on nearby Shemya. With these two air bases, Kiska would be isolated from Japan and could either be starved or frozen out – or easily conquered – as Washington might elect.

The decision: This would be a joint Army/Navy expedition with Rear Admiral Francis E. Rockwell in command of amphibious forces. Major General Albert E. Brown of the 7th Division would lead the troops on shore.

There had been strong division at the planning level meetings held in San Diego. Each "side" had their vested interests and when it was decided to bring in the 7th Division rather than use troops already in Alaska – the Alaska troops were untrained in amphibious landings among other limitations – strong resistance was voiced about using General Brown. The General was from South Carolina, had no northern experience and he declined to make a "recon" trip to the Aleutians to see what he was getting into. Nor would General Brown accept as Second-in-Command General Landrum whom, we will recall, was a member of Buckner's staff and "knew" the Aleutians.

General DeWitt, an administrator, made a pronouncement that with 500 defenders on Attu (Kinkaid's official estimate), the

(Opposite page) Battleship *Pennsylvania* issues salvo from 14-inch guns at Attu. (Above) *Pennsylvania* as viewed from OS2U Kingfisher scout airplane.

island could be captured in three days. General Brown wanted a week. There are those who feel the War Department gave the go-ahead on the basis that only one Division would be needed for the beaches, but a second division, Buckner's 4th, would be on "alert-reserve" at Adak only 24 hours away. The time estimate by DeWitt, "three days," was what Washington wanted to hear

Earlier mention was made that Colonel Eareckson was not in on the Amchitka first plane landing as he was away on "Buckner business." It was Eareckson who presented Air Force views at the San Diego meeting. Regrettably, so the benefit of 20-20 hindsight illustrates, the planners did not accept very much of the input from men who had been soldiering in Alaska and specifically in the Aleutians.

Brown didn't want to confuse his command by adding Buckner's men even though Buckner (who by now had been promoted to Lt. General), admonished, "You'll need them. The Infantry will have to go in there with cork-screws to dig out the Japanese."

Near the last minute, Admiral Kinkaid submitted revisions on estimated strength at Attu up from 500 to 1,600 based on the

Liberation Day for Attu May 11, 1943 when American troops stormed Japanese entrenched on island.

latest aerial photograph interpretations. With this new intelligence General Brown said he would probably need all of his ,7th Infantry in addition to Buckner's reinforcements – 10,000 men. The calendar told the staff it had less than three weeks to put it all together, thus the "we can't do that" attitude changed over night to possibility thinking. The assault was committed and those in command would have to see that it was successful.

Admiral Rockwell needed ships. Admiral Nimitz recognized this and assigned battleships U.S.S. *Pennsylvania, Idaho* and *Nevada*; escort carrier *Nassau*; new light cruiser *Santa Fe* (which had replaced *Salt Lake City* which was at Mare Island for overhaul) and cruiser *Detroit.* Only destroyer, *Coghlan,* from the Komondorski operation, was still in the picture as all the others had been sent out to get fixed. Five new destroyers were added.

To thwart any spies who might be lurking, false sailing orders were published and medical officers announced almost publicly, that talks were scheduled on "tropical diseases." Although navigation charts of the coast of Argentina were left in obvious places, the secret orders called for the rendezvous to be at a place most had never heard of: Cold Bay.

At Attu: General Buckner (left) discusses status of battle with officers near end of campaign.

When all was assembled, the destroyer pack had risen from half-a-dozen to 19. There were four attack transports for the 7th Division, and DeWitt had chartered the passenger liner S.S. *Perida* to haul the 4th Infantry Division.

The advance force of submarines undersea, and PBY patrol bombers oversea, plus McMorris' cruisers and destroyers, were on full alert patrolling in case any Japanese shipping or aircraft ventured into the area. Even with the three battle wagons on patrol west of Attu, the Japanese managed to slip *Kimikawa Maru*, a tender, with light escorts, into Attu to unload some scout planes. The greatest threat, however, was as usual, the weather. This caused the invasion of Attu to be canceled twice and the troops kept cooped up on the transports at sea

D-Day for Attu was May 11, 1943. Between 3 and 5 a.m., giant submarines *Narwhal* and *Nautilus* each put 100 Alaska Scouts ashore for a pre-landing beach search. Destroyer *Kane* landed 400 reconnaissance troops a few hours later. By nightfall, about 1,500 troops were on "Beach Red" just outside Holtz Bay. Other troops landed near Massacre Bay and by 8 p.m. about 2,000 were ashore. No Japanese were seen but they were there.

Colonel Yamazaki decided not to waste his men or his ammunition trying to defend the beaches. He had only 2,630 men, 12 anti-aircraft guns and some artillery – grossly inadequate for knocking out any landing party. He would employ delaying tactics and make the price of liberating Attu very dear for the Americans.

DeWitt's "three days" and Brown's "week" would have to be extended considerably longer. The greatest tragedy was that many American troops would undergo near starvation due to inability to move supplies. The soggy Muskeg bogged vehicles of all kinds. The foggy weather bogged down troops. It was bitter cold for men who had trained in Southern California for the African desert then been ordered to Alaska with improper clothing and improper boots neither of which would keep out the cold. Forty-eight hours on the beach and the advance had been only 4,000 yards.

General Brown blamed the terrain. He blamed the greater enemy strength than he said he had been led to anticipate. He was overheard predicting it would require half a year to conquer the desolate island. All of Brown's negativism was enough for General John L. DeWitt. Two days later General Brown was fired. General Landrum, DeWitt's earlier choice of commandants, replaced him.

The pursuit of the Japanese indeed required cork-screwing them out one at a time. With far superior numbers, the American forces overcame resistance first at Holtz Bay, then to just about

Continued on page 118

106

General Eugene Landrum at Attu. First American flag on Attu was raised above old Japanese harbor boat.

(Below) The boggy tundra mired down vehicles leaving no other choice than for the soldiers had to hand-carry supplies. See photo page 110.

Unloading small boats at Attu. (Lower) Abandoned Japanese landing barge.

Handcars pushed by Japanese soldiers along-side airstrip construction site. Japanese tractor, shot full of holes on Attu. (Lower) American tent city springs up a week after landings.

American truck (top) stuck-in-the-mud, Attu. (Lower) Corps of Engineers haul trailer of supplies up gravel-bottom creek for better traction than over tundra.

My outfit was lucky on Attu. Only 2 killed, 2 hurt but Lt. Cedric Tallis was shot in the helmet knocking him woozy for awhile. Tallis was later Vice Pres of N.Y. Yankees. We watched the stupid Japs jumping off the hills into Massacre Bay rather than being taken prisoner. —Mack Mark , M Co. 71st Inf. Canoga Park, Calif.

Troops became stevedores for hauling supplies at Uniktali Bay, near Dutch Harbor. (Lower) For sanitation, U.S. troops "policed" Attu: "If it isn't growing, pick it up."

THESE MEN MADE ATTU LANDING

BULLETS FLY CLOSE TO ACS MEN AT ATTU

ATTU—"...Occasionally a sniper's bullet would ricochet close by. A number of Japs remained in foxholes dug into the hills on each side of the valley, flanking us. Toward nightfall we watched our machine guns rout them out. Two of the snipers were spilled and rolled, over and over, down snow banks to the bottom of the hill.

"It was an indelible introduction."

That's the way Lt. Lawrence Bucy, Attu OIC, describes the first day the ACS task force was ashore here setting up a temporary station.

"Moving our equipment, plus two drums of gasoline and 10 gallons of oil taken off the beach, to the temporary site was a difficult task," he re-

ATTU—Here's the Attu honor roll—the ACS men who played their part in the conquest of the first American territory to be retaken in this war.

Lts. Lawrence W. Bucy and William Greene; WO Kenneth K. Hillmon; M/Sgt. John W. Huff; S/Sgt. W. D. Canfield and Dewaine Hardin*; Sgt. Howard Brice*; T/4s Leonard Back, Thomas Carr, William Partee, Maynard Petersen and Clinton Stockley; T/5

Ernest Naef; PFCs G.I. Counter and Elmer Jones, and Pvts. John Catanese, Stanley Hedlund and Dennis Murphy. Cpl. Carl Loy, in the original group, was assigned to accompany station material on another vessel and didn't arrive here until combat ceased. (Men pictured not in order listed.)
*Later promoted to T/Sgt.
—(U.S. Army Signal Corps Photos.)

BULLETS FLY CLOSE TO ACS MEN AT ATTU

ATTU—"...Occasionally a sniper's bullet would ricochet close by. A number of Japs remained in foxholes dug into the hills on each side of the valley, flanking us. Toward nightfall we watched our machine guns rout them out. Two of the snipers were spilled and rolled, over and over, down snow banks to the bottom of the hill.

"It was an indelible introduction."

That's the way Lt. Lawrence Bucy, Attu OIC, de-

(Continued next page)

scribes the first day the ACS task force was a-
shore here setting up a temporary station.

"Moving our equipment, plus two drums of gasoline and 10 gallons of oil taken off the beach, to
the temporary site was a difficult task," he recalled, "even with a tractor and trailer. All of
us thought the work ahead looked endless.

"Lt.Col. Irwin L. Kaufman, ADC Signal Officer,
helped load the trailer, and like the rest, pushed
when the going got tough. We were able to get the
equipment and supplies to within about 150 yards
of the site with the tractor. The evening was occupied carrying tents and K rations up the hill to
the site and digging in.

"The operations tent was dug in first. Personnel slept partly on boards we managed to bring
from the beach, and partly on muddy ground inside
the tents.

"We were up at daybreak to begin packing in gen-
erators and the sets. While several of the men
were eating K ration breakfast, the Japs aimed
some 37 mm shells our way. One burst directly over our fire. None of our men was wounded, but a
fragment of the shell struck a man from another u-
nit a short distance away, in the foot.

"During the combat period and for two full
months it was necessary to keep a four-man guard
during the eight hours of the night. Operators
worked eight to 10 hours at the sets, plus any
other necessary labor and guard duty. Within a
week after the landing we had carried enough lumber to floor two personnel tents and a mess tent.
#

NO GOLDEN, SUN-KISSED SANDS, THESE:—Nope, it's the beach at Shemya, with Captain Murray's original landing group. Landing craft in background. FRONT (left to right): M/Sgt. Malcolm Morrison; M/Sgt. Larry Davenport; T/3 Alfred T. Vaughan; Cpl. Vincent E. Hagen; Murray; T/Sgt. Dorward E. Strong; Pvt. Stieg W. Gabrielson; T/5 Warren W. Adams; T/5 Ronald R. Campbell. REAR: S/Sgt. Harold E. Leise; T/4 Edward F. Cavanaugh; Pvt. Daniel L. Ruthford; Cpl. Joseph A. Yucas; T/4 Frank M. Glantz; Sgt. Albert O. Wickstrom; T/5 Robert D. Schiller.—(U.S.Signal Corps Photo.)

Alaska Communications System Signal Corps troops of all ranks moved themselves and tons of equipment ashore on Attu (left page) and on Shemya (this page).

Abandoned Japanese artillery on Attu. (Lower) Fire at Chichagof Harbor caused by U.S. bombers.

Attu: Inhospitable in winter snow or in summer fog.

On going in to Chichagof Pass we were shelled for about 45 minutes and I said my prayers frontwards, backwards and upside down. Some fellow said he wanted to say the rosary but had lost his beads. He did not know how to pray. —Stan Wall. 7th Inf. Attu
Oak Lawn, Ill

G.I.'s probed tents with fixed bayonets (top)one-at-a-time on Attu looking for Japanese. (Lower) American soldiers look with anguish at corpses of Japanese soldiers on Attu.

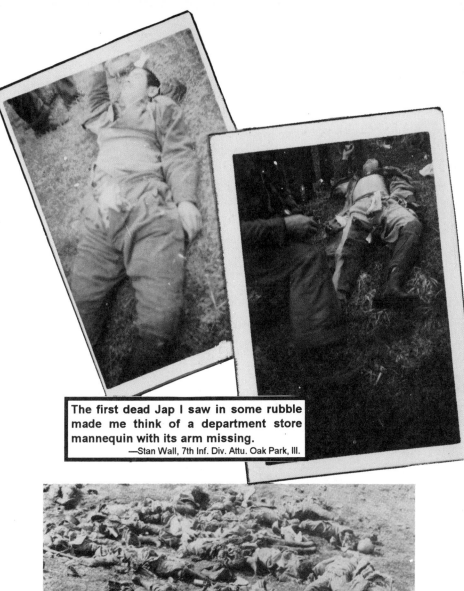

The first dead Jap I saw in some rubble made me think of a department store mannequin with its arm missing.
—Stan Wall, 7th Inf. Div. Attu. Oak Park, Ill.

Tenno heika banzai – "May the Emperor live 10,000 years."

(Continued from page 106)

everyone's surprise in a ten days period, May 19-29, the Japanese
flew in some twin-engine BETTY bombers from Paramushiro.
Several were promptly lost to P-38's. The Imperial Navy, not
wanting to risk what was left of their Navy to superior American
forces, and bad weather, abandoned the Army garrison and stayed
at Paramushiro.

The Japanese on Attu made a gallant but fatal 1,000-man
banzai charge on the early morning of the 29th. Some of these
desperate soldiers roared through a hospital tent stabbing
American wounded and killed a Lt. Colonel while over-running
two command posts. They were finally halted by an American
Army Engineer Detachment. In their final desperate moments,
about 500 Japanese soldiers killed themselves with hand grenades.

These soldiers huddled in groups of about half-a-dozen,
shouted the *banzai* to the Emperor then one of them pulled the pin
of a grenade and dropped it on the ground in the center of the
huddle. American soldiers were startled at the mass of shattered
corpses and had the chore of burying them.

—The Attu, Alaska Campaign—
The Battle on Attu Was the First American Liberation
of Japanese-Seized American Territory in the Pacific War

	Americans	Japanese
Dead	552*	2,35
Wounded	1,140	0**
Prisoners	0	28

* The U.S. Army did not announce a final count
** None captured by the U.S. Wounded Japanese were believed to
have been killed by comrades or committed suicide

Lessons learned on Attu served the Americans well in later
invasions throughout the Pacific Theater.

The Japanese High Command had ordered an evacuation of the
Attu garrison but canceled the operation when it heard broadcasts
that an invasion had started. Except for the 28 prisoners taken, all
Japanese troops died to the last man. (Some of the prisoners had
been hiding in caves and a number of them came out at night to
steal food from the American field kitchens.)

These deaths included Paul Tatsuguchi, MD, who had been

schooled in California and forced into Imperial service while he was serving in a medical mission in Japan for the Seventh Day Adventist Church.

In Washington, the Navy kept *silent* about the invasion at Attu for four days. But Tokyo Rose kept those within earshot of her broadcasts well informed even though her information was colorfully inaccurate.

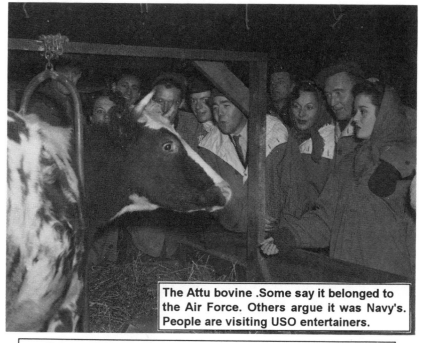

The Attu bovine .Some say it belonged to the Air Force. Others argue it was Navy's. People are visiting USO entertainers.

Commodore Gehres' Flight Surgeon suggested with tongue in cheek that the staff officers would be more healthy if they had fresh milk and eggs. So the Commodore sent the U.S.S. *Teal*, a seaplane tender, to Whidby Island to fetch a cow and some chickens.
—Robert W. Jensen, Navy. Portland, Oregon

We had been on a patrol in *S-42* out of Attu looking for targets between there and Paramushiro. We didn't find any. It was a 38-day cruise in ice water. We had been back a few days when the aft batteries blew up. I was the cook and on deck but some below were hurt.
—Leon Sheppard. *S-42* Hurst, Texas

Welcome! TO ALEXAI POINT
...UNINCORPORATED...
THE HOME OF THE ARMY'S
NORTHWESTERN ~ MOST
..AIRFIELD..

FOUNDED
JUNE-8-1943
ELEVATION 15 FT.

BUILT BY THE
ENGINEERS

POPULATION
MALE Censored MILITARY SECRET
FEMALE — 0

(Opposite page - top) Wrecked Japanese airplane well picked over for souvenirs. P-38 (center) left scratches in brand new steel runway. (Lower) Air Operations officers (l to r) Lts. Bill Macbeth, Coon, Hedeen. (This page) Digging out remains of collapsed building after snow storm – Shemya. Snow-cat by Studebaker, (lower) grunted its way along on Shemya.

Major Jack Chennault, Air Force fighter plane leader with his P-40. (lower) This P-40 ran out of gas, landed on beach. Pilot walked away.

The Army chartered a local fishing barge to move troops to Port Heiden. Note First World War helmets. Only a handful of men had cork life jackets. (Lower) There was very little entertainment in this outfit other than the dart board on wall and the self-made music played by ear.

Chapter 17
Scenes From Shemya

The Japanese were thinking of occupying Shemya as a protection to nearly Kiska. But the Americans got there first which increased the stress-level of all those on Kiska.

Anti-aircraft guns were set up on Shemya to ward off bomb runs from nearby Kiska. (Lower) The winter of 1943-1944 on Shemya. It was a challenge to even try to be comfortable in a tent at 0° F.

MIKE MARK

SHEMYA — 1943

No harbor, no docks on
Shemya caused heavy
going for unloading
everything from trucks to
C rations. (Lower) Shemya
"residential neighbor-
hood" summer 1944.

125

First World War Flying Ace Eddie Rickenbacker visits Shemya as combination morale booster and official observer on progress of the war. He wrote "The Aleutian Islands was our coldest and dreariest military front, closer to Japan than to the continental United States. We had to stay there to keep the Japanese out."

Olivia deHaviland, Academy Award winning movie actress, arrived on Shemya in a C-47 with bucket seats. Her visit inspired the troops to win the war by hard work so everyone could go home.

126

Runway at Shemya. It was first steel, later concrete. (Lower) P-38 skidded out of its element when it plowed dirt off the edge of the metal air strip.

This P-38 skidded out of its element and plowed dirt off edge of metal runway.

127

"Bad Luck" in the Aleutians

(Top to bottom) P-40 of RCAF; American P-39; American very flyable but obsolete B-18A; Shemya airport's control tower.

PBY5A Catalina parked at end of Shemya's steel runway. (Lower) Marsdon steel runway rolled up like wall paper in howling winter storm.

Metamorphoses of the "chamber." Early edition, later addition.

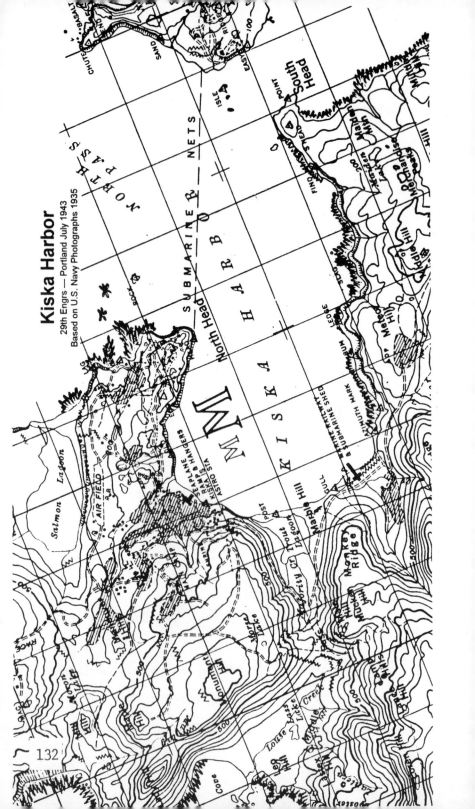

Kiska Harbor

29th Engrs — Portland July 1943
Based on U.S. Navy Photographs 1935

Chapter 18
"Get Kiska Back"

For any who are unfamiliar with the outcome of the sorties and battles of the Aleutian islands and who are reading about them for the first time here, let us acknowledge that the Japanese Government, which found itself between a rock and a hard place at Kiska, did have a choice: either watch the total annihilation of its men on Kiska, as they had been forced to do at Attu, or pull off a clandestine operation of "rescue." Getting their troops off Kiska between American bombings, and using the heavy fog to cover the evacuation, would be a challenge not only with the timing but with "lady luck" herself.

The Japanese had removed thousands of troops from Guadalcanal in early February 1943 by running in as many as 20 destroyers over about a week's time. Admiral Nimitz declared, "Only skill in keeping their plans disguised and bold celerity in carrying them out enabled the withdrawal [to succeed]."

It has been said that a difficult task once accomplished is easier done a second time. Recognizing their success in removing well over 10,000 troops while meeting American offensives on Guadalcanal, where there wasn't any freezing weather, blinding fog and "williwaws," could the Japanese use the elements of weather to hide an evacuation at Kiska? We will look at this shortly.

Even while the battle for the liberation of Attu was in progress, Colonel Talley of the engineers was busy only 25 miles from Kiska putting in an airstrip on Shemya. Object: construct an airport on which to base the new B-29 Super-fort bombers for raid's on the Japanese home islands. In spite of very wild weather, the job progressed with the 18th Engineers at work and elements of the 4th Infantry as "guards."

Planners at work for upcoming liberation of Kiska. (Seated) Rear Adm. Rockwell; Vice Adm. Kinkaid; Maj. Gen. Corlett; Lt. Gen. Buckner; Maj. Gen. Butler; Maj. Gen. Pearkes (Canada).

On Attu, even while the shooting was still going on, other elements of American engineers went to work on an airport there. While the Japanese construction crews had been forced to use mostly pick-and-shovel methods, Col. Talley moved in heavy equipment and had an all-new site (he didn't like the location chosen by the Japanese), cleared and ready for traffic on Alexai Point by June 8th. Only days later the basic strip at Shemya was completed.

The Japanese on Kiska were now in the middle with American aircraft east of them as well as one to the west. In addition, the U.S. Navy put in a submarine servicing base at Attu. To force the pincers, General Buckner sent troops to occupy Rat Island nearby.

The heat of emotions was getting to both Kinkaid and to Buckner. Each wanted a strong base in the Aleutians as their personal jumping off place for attacks on Japan. The Joint Chiefs in Washington agreed.

Now with a shooting war on American soil – Alaska's far-flung islands – money flowed down the Aleutian chain like oil from an uncapped well. The Navy at Pearl Harbor ordered major battle wagons into northern waters. Days of the "Kiska Blitz" were recalled as the Air Force resumed bombings and strafings on a heavy schedule.

The Japanese managed to slip in some ships and also reinforced the garrison by submarine. From at least one, some significant cargo was unloaded: RADAR!

The Japanese were ingenious in their technological developments but their success with the development of RADAR was not one of them. (Eventually the Germans would send RADAR sets to Japan and they would install RADAR on some Japanese submarines voyaging between Japan and Europe.) Even with the primitive RADAR installed at Kiska, the anti-aircraft fire became more intense and more deadly than ever before. But time was running out and the Japanese knew it.

The U.S. Naval blockade of Kiska, and the incessant pounding of the aircraft, was successful in keeping nearly all supply missions for Kiska away. Realizing that the end of their occupation days was at hand, Japan decided to bring in *I*-class submarines to secretly take off the garrison. But submarines only handle a limited number of passengers. They are expensive and losses had been high.

PC-487, a little U.S. Navy picket boat, located *I-24* near Shemya by sonar. After heaving five depth charges into the sea that severely damaged *I-24*, the submarine suddenly bobbed to the surface. Lt. William G. Cornell rammed the submarine, put about and crashed it again this time making a huge hole in the conning tower. Meanwhile, the boat's machine guns and 3-incher peppered the enemy submarine unmercifully. Out of control and taking water rapidly, *I-24* sank with all hands.

U.S.S. *Frazier*, a destroyer, made contact with *I-31* immediately after the submarine had loaded evacuees at Kiska and was heading for Japan. *I-31* did not survive Frazier's attack and went down with all hands and all of its passengers.

I-7 lost an "argument" with American destroyer, *Monaghan*, which had been working the Aleutians ever since the start of affairs there. Commander Nagai was running on the surface nearing the end of a rough passage from Paramushiro when the destroyer's RADAR plotted the sub's position. With a carefully placed salvo, *Monaghan's* gunners knocked the conning tower off the submarine's hull but the sub keep headway, operated from the below-deck control room, and managed to get to Kiska to unload cargo. But plans had to be scrapped to evacuate personnel as the submarine could not submerge without sinking. Although the crew tried to run for Japan a few days later, the submarine was shelled again by *Monaghan* thus forcing *I- 7* to ground itself. Some writers claim the crew scuttled the big attack submarine, others say American bombers broke it up on the beach.

Statistics against removing the Kiska garrison by submarine were being counted:

I-24	**Sunk with all hands**
I-31	**Sunk with all hands and evacuees—**
	about 300 men
I-7	**Sunk. Some survivors**

Still over 5,000 men on Kiska to be evacuated.

The American Navy brought in cruisers, more destroyers and returned several S-boats to Aleutian waters and subjected Kiska to heavy shelling. From his home base on Paramushiro, Admiral Kawase notified Tokyo that if the garrison at Kiska was to be salvaged, some immediate attention, other than with submarines, was urgent.

Very quietly and as quickly as a plan could be devised, the Japanese sent a fleet of three cruisers (*Tama, Abukuma, Kiso)* along with a screen of destroyers to get their men off Kiska. The plan was a bold one – steam right into the harbor, hopefully under fog, fetch the men and scoot out* shooting up U.S. forces along the way if any should be encountered.

The U.S. also brought up a fleet as though preparing for an invasion. Ships added to the Northern force in the Aleutians included battleships *Idaho, Mississippi* and *New Mexico.* There were also the cruisers *Louisville, Portland, San Francisco, Santa Fe and Wichita.* In addition, there were nine destroyers.

On July 22, 1943, these ships found Kiska bathed in brilliant sunlight and immediately opened up with salvos of 14-inch shells

*See chapter: "How the Japanese Did It."

136

from battleships and with 5- and 6-inch shells from the cruisers. At the end of the shelling the U.S. force retired to refuel. With the advantage of hindsight, it would now seem to have been a better plan to have left a couple of ships at the scene as scouts.

Although neither side had seen the other's ships, the Japanese evacuation force crossed the very area where only hours earlier the American battleships had been during the shelling. But all the Japanese ships didn't get to Kiska due to the usual problem: the weather!

We recall Admiral "Fuzzy" Theobald's incident wherein he set out to attack Kiska but with the collision of some of his ships in the pea-soup fog, he aborted his plan and went back to Kodiak. In the Japanese fog-bound mishap, several ships crunched, two so badly smashed they could not participate in the evacuation plans. They were ordered to carefully turn around and to splash their way back to the body shop in the Kuriles. The remainder of the force proceeded to Kiska by a round-about route.

Off Kiska the fog had thickened. With one destroyer posted as guard, and two other destroyers doing harbor entrance patrol, the rest of the fleet entered Kiska's harbor where the garrison had been working feverishly, between American and Canadian bombings, to blow up every installation in a great attempt to render the island as a junk yard gift to the Americans. This effort was most successful as our photographs illustrate.

As the cruiser and destroyer rescue ships came in, the men on shore, many of whom had been waiting on the beach for days, were told to abandon everything, even their rifles (which they threw into the bay) as space on the ships was too short. In less than one hour, all 5,183 men were taken aboard. The Japanese ships hauled out quickly, did a reverse of their round-about route then headed for Paramushiro without having fired a shot. All docked there without any losses and without having seen or been seen by the Americans.

In less than 1 hour, on July 28, 1943, the Japanese evacuated all 5,183 men from Kiska without mishap then returned to Paramushiro without firing a shot and without being seen by the U.S. Navy.

Armada readies in Adak Harbor for Kiska invasion. (Lower)
Landing craft have left transports and head for Kiska beach.

Chapter 19
Kiska Invaded – Nobody Home

D-Day for Kiska was August 15, 1943. For this event, a great armada assembled in the harbor at Adak. More American ships arrived to take part including the battleship *Tennessee* with its four destroyers. Every officer and crewman expected to do battle.

In the meantime, General Buckner was becoming suspicious about lack of Japanese activity at Kiska. His airmen were coming back with reports that the previously devastating anti-aircraft fire over Kiska was missing. They said all had been quiet there for several days. American authorities wondered if the enemy could be sitting it out in their massive underground "city"? Or, could they have evacuated? Buckner knew about the Guadalcanal evacuation, the news of which took five days to reach the Americans who were on the same island.

Based on an intensive study of aerial photographs, Admiral Kinkaid knew the island was heavily fortified. Accordingly, he decided to proceed with an invasion in event the silence was later determined to be that the enemy was hiding in caves just waiting for a landing force. He also looked closely at the lessons of Attu and made up his mind there would be no shortage of troops, no bottle necks at the beach and above all, no shortage of food. His force would be headed by Major General Charles H. Corlett, former commander of the Army's Fort Greely at Kodiak. A Canadian unit would be led by Brigadier General H. W. Foster of the Canadian Army, Pacific Command. Rear Admiral Francis W. Rockwell, U.S.N., would handle Navy interests and be responsible for landing the troops.

Admiral Kinkaid was overall commander. General Buckner would be there. But Kinkaid would have some back-seat drivers in the persons of none other than Lt. General John L. DeWitt, Commanding General of the Western Defense Command and 4th Army, who finally got away from his desk in San Francisco and

> The Post Quartermaster Bakery at Fort Greely was ordered to bake bread, it seemed like tons of loaves of white, somewhat thick crusted bread, before each action down the chain. This bread was sealed in waxed paper wrappers on wrapping machines brought in from a commercial bakery in Seattle. We stacked the bread in cabbage crates for shipping. While we were baking bread, all the usual pastry items, even doughnuts, were discontinued. We baked bread 24-hours a day for days.
>
> —Bart K. M. Murdoch, QM Bkry Det.
> Savannah, Georgia

Troops Involved

7th Infantry Division (some were Attu veterans)	15,000
4th Infantry Regiment	5,000
87th Mountain Combat team (trained for Italy)	5,000
13th Canadian Infantry Brigade 5,300	
1st Special Service (paratroops commando guerrilla)	2,500
Signal, Medical, Quartermaster and special personnel	1,626
	34,426

Major General Howland M. "Howlin' Mad" Smith, Marine Corps observer.

At this point, the joint Chiefs of Staff were quietly considering the Aleutians as the jumping off place for direct attacks on the Japanese home islands. With this in mind, it seemed appropriate to have a "Washingtonian" as observer. This would be Assistant Secretary of War John J. McCloy. McCloy was anxious to participate He was issued a steel helmet and other paraphernalia and went along.

General Corlett's troops became known as "Corlett's Long Knives." He issued a booklet to each soldier while they were on the transports, the book pointing out that everyone must work together, officers and men alike "while we are fighting the Japs." The foreword in the book was signed:

Sincerely and respectfully yours
Charles H. Corlett, Major General, A. U. S., Commanding.

Friday the 13th was a date to remember! On that date, over 100 ships left Adak for their rendezvous with the Japanese at Kiska. Two days later a patrol of Alaska Scouts, followed by the Mountain Infantry, landed on one side of the island while the main force headed for a beach on the west side.

THE LONG KNIVES

Cover and page 1 from General Corlett's *Soldier's Manual* for "conduct of the war" on Kiska. (Lower) Air Force Col. Eareckson wrote the words for Corlett's fight song.

Major General Charles H. Corlett as Commanding General at Fort Greely. He later led liberation of Kiska, invasion of Kwajalein, was planner for Normandy Invasion. He had a nickname "Cowboy Pete." Note field telephone hung with big nail, example of early communications and Spartan office at Fort Greely.

The first of the Alaska Scouts ashore was the commander, Colonel William J. Verbeck, who immediately suspected "nobody home" when he and his group came upon an abandoned gun position near the beach. Everywhere they went they found devastation – destroyed war materiel but no Japanese. When the first of over 7, 000 troops swarmed ashore, Navy Ensign William C. Jones was among them. He hadn't been there but a few minutes when one of several stray dogs singled him out, raced to him and greeted him with typical puppy-enthusiasm: Explosion! The puppy he'd left with the Navy weather crew 15 months before had survived life with the Japanese, all the shelling and bombings and remembered him.

Three days later, General Corlett messaged the joint Chiefs of Staff that there was no enemy on Kiska. With no Japanese to shoot at, trigger-happy invading Americans and Canadians had managed to shoot at each other apparently due to the fog. This invasion on a "nobody's home" island produced 313 casualties. Of this number 24 had been shot, four were killed by mines or bobby-traps and over 100 picked up trench foot and there were miscellaneous injuries. Of the Canadians: 4 were dead, 4 had been injured, and the Canadians suffered one case of trench foot.

The U.S. Navy also had losses. Destroyer *Abner Read* hit a mine left behind by the Japanese which broke off the stern killing 71. Wounded and missing numbered 47.

General Corlett posted orders. One order was to comb every

(Continued on page 148)

Some of Kiska's "quiet" guns. Top two photos made in 1987.

143

"All ashore who's going ashore" for the liberation of Kiska. Transport is U.S.A.T. *Grant*

(Top), Kiska harbor and wrecked *Nojima Maru*. (Center) Landing beach. Note two broken Japanese 2-man subs. (Lower) Hospital tent on Kiska's beach.

145

Japanese had 5, 2-man submarines at Kiska. Three on marine railway, two on beach. Lower two photos made 1987.

CAPTURED JAP SUB BASE ON KISKA - OFFICIAL PHOTO

The U. S. Navy hauled away all but two of the 2-man subs discovered at Kiska. Picture at right made in 1989.

(Continued from page 142)

inch of the island and search every cave. Another was to build an airport immediately. This job went to Colonel Talley.

> (The Japanese tried to make a hey-day in their press. They claimed the Americans had invaded an abandoned, isolated, weather-beaten Kiska Island which tied up hundreds of thousands of troops throughout Alaska that otherwise would have been used against them in the South Pacific.)

John J. McCloy went back to Washington, D.C. disappointed at not being in on a fighting invasion, nevertheless excited for having been aboard. General DeWitt, disappointed at not seeing any battle, went back to his desk in the Presidio of San Francisco. His "active theater" was deactivated with the landings on Kiska and the Aleutian "headache" came to an end.

*   *   *

We have seen that for decades Alaska got almost nothing in money to develop military effectiveness, but once the threat of a shooting war was exposed, funds became available. Concrete runways replaced tundra. Steel Quonset huts and later permanent buildings replaced native drift-wood-and-sod shacks, and hundreds of thousands of men moved in. But the cold and unfriendly weather – fog caused by a mix of cold from the Bering Sea and warm from the extension of *Kuroshio,* was a leading excuse to base the B-29 raids on the Japanese home islands from the Mariana Islands instead of from the concrete and steel airport on Shemya. A lone B-29, on a trial run, and also to worry the Japanese, touched down on Shemya but it did not stay.

Some of the Aleutian outposts became of strategic importance in the cold-war with the Soviet Union. For awhile, Northwest Orient Airlines, the first commercial airline to operate from Seattle-Tacoma International Airport to Okinawa using 4-engine Lockheed Constellations and DC-7's, had a fueling stop at Shemya. Now that pure jets, Boeing 747s, Douglas DC-10s, etc. make the Orient flights, if fuel is needed, a top-off is obtained at Anchorage International Airport.

Fort Greely, which sprang to life during the tense months before Pearl Harbor on Kodiak, was closed – torn down – the site today looks like a vacant lot. But the post's name was moved to a new site 91 miles northwest of Fairbanks.

The naval station on Woman's Bay, Kodiak, is presently a major Coast Guard Search and Rescue installation. The Navy still maintains a major base at Adak but since the demise of the Soviet Union, its importance seems on the decline. Amchitka became an under-ground nuclear testing facility. Over at Atka, the natives returned and rebuilt their village. Kiska is abandoned and although some salvage efforts were attempted, photos made in the late 1980's show Kiska still resembles a gigantic junk pile remaining from the Japanese occupation and the Kiska Blitz.

When the Japanese seized Kiska they came to stay. Their first act was to rename it Narukami-shima. Then they installed a system of fire hydrants. Photograph made in 1987.

When General Corlett was named Commanding General for the liberation of Kiska, he decided to have full motion picture documentation so arranged for professional cinematographer. Flags on Kiska: Americans arrive; Japanese went home.

Japanese monument to downed American pilot. (Center
and lower) Japanese caves in mountainsides.

Alaska Communications System Quonset hut was buried during winter storm. (Center) ACS complex, Kiska. The censor cut off top of picture as it showed the harbor in background. (Lower) Steel arrives so operations can be moved from tents to Quonset Huts. The ASC men did their own installations.

PASSED BY
U 02833 S
ARMY EXAMINER

Post Censor

Winter on Kiska. Lt. Clare Hanawalt, Alaska Communications System, in fur-lined parka. Censor approved the photo so he could send it home.

Recreation for service personnel on Kiska included ski instruction from a visiting Norwegian expert. (Lower) Results of half-a-day's fishing expedition on Kiska.

Mysterious, little known, very cold, Bering Sea as viewed from Shemya on a rare "good" day.

The Wildlife Service has traditionally kept an eye on the fox population in the Aleutians and on poachers. Shown is a rare albino Blue Fox on Kiska.

155

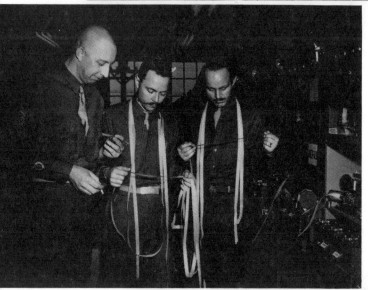

"Get the Message Through" was motto of Alaska Communications System. (Top photos both pages) Portion of bank of teletype perforators and printers for high-speed transmission of messages at Kiska. (Left page) Signal Corps technicians inspect perforated tape. Mascot poses as if reading from teletype. (This page) rolls of submarine cable that was soon planted between Kiska and Adak to carry messages and telephone calls. (Lower) The major communications method was by Morse Code. Operator with hidden right hand probably on telegraph key. Due to shortage of radios, many different brands were acquired.

Scuba Diver braved frigid water of Kiska Harbor to see what the Japanese left behind: Shell casings, bottles, unused bullets, junk. On next page the diver located a Coke bottle undoubtedly from "flying-glass splinter-bombs" originated by Col. Eareckson

who had crewmen in bombers throw cases of empty Coke and
beer bottles out the open bomb bay doors. Kiska harbor in 1987
where the dilapidated war-time U. S. Army dock was used for
visitor's boat. Note *Nojima Maru* stuck hard in sand for nearly 50
years; Japanese anti-aircraft guns on bluff.

Shemya

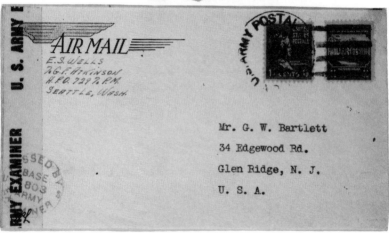

E. S. Wells, a civilian, worked for Guy F. Atkinson Construction Company on Shemya and his mail was subject to military censorship. How he managed to get seldom used 4½¢ and 1½¢ stamps way out at Shemya is anyone's guess. The total 6¢ paid airmail postage.

The covers (envelopes) illustrated here are run-of-the-mill types found in all collections of postal historians and were selected for use here trying to find an example of each APO that operated in the Aleutians. We were partially successful. None is of more than of minimal value to a collector but the various postmarks and CENSOR marks provide an historical record of what war-time mail half-a-century ago looked like.

Chapter 20
Mail for Troops in Alaska; The A.P.O.

It took awhile for the Army Post Office to get set up but once it became active, mail moved with as much efficiency to the APO's as it did between cities "state-side."

In Alaska, before the Army Postal Service arrived, mail passed through several offices sometimes with pretty fair service but other times a description of the service could easily be classed as "horrible."

The author's experience was unique because he was in the right places at the right time therefore is able to recall pre-war as well as after-war started mail handling.

On arrival at Kodiak in July 1941, six months before war was declared and before the army that established there was named Fort Greely, an address was simply:

Rank and name of soldier -- serial number
Branch of Service
Army Expeditionary Force
Kodiak, Alaska

This soon changed to rank, name, serial number, name of outfit and Fort Greely, Kodiak Alaska. This later evolved to rank, name, serial number, a special designation for the outfit, as in the Signal Corps this was simply "S-1," followed by Fort Greely, Kodiak, Alaska. (In the smaller units, as ours, that started with 15 men and never grew beyond about 40, the address was simplified. An example of this appears in the illustrations.) Finally a format was decided upon to be used world-wide as:

Rank and name -- serial number
Organization
APO 000
c/o Postmaster at designated stateside city

📬 APOs – Anchorage to Attu
Official Post Office records are not complete for some dates

APO	Geographic Location	Military Name	Start	Close
942	Anchorage	Ft. Richardson	Mar 1 42	?- 1948
937	Kodiak	Ft. Greely	May 13 42	May 15 46
944	Cold Bay	Ft. Randall	Apr 3 42	Oct 31 53
939	Dutch Harbor	Ft. Mears	Apr 17 42	?- 1948
948	Umnak	Ft. Glenn	May 16 42	May 1 59
983	Atka	—	Oct ? 42	Oct 18 45
980	Adak	Hq. 11th AF	Aug 3 42	Jul 8 50
730	Adak	(other troops)	Aug 8 43	Oct 31 44
986*	Tanaga	—	Nov 1 42	— ?
986*	Amchitka	—	Mar 1 43	Jan 14 51
730**	Kiska	—	Aug 17 43	Oct 31 44
986-1**	Kiska	—	Nov 1 44	Oct 31 45
729	Shemya	—***	Jun 10 43	Aug 2 54
726	Attu	Camp Earle	May 23 43	Dec 31 47

* Tanaga and Amchitka shared the same APO.
** Kiska's APO 730 was original assignment but was renumbered 986-1 on reorganization.
***Jocularly called "Ft. Junkpile" due to mountains of wrecked Japanese equipment.
—Source: Shafer, James. *Geographic Locations of U.S. APOs 1941-1984* War Cover Club. 1985.

In the pre-war era – about six months – mail came by ship from Seattle and was off-loaded at the naval base at Woman's Bay. This is about 6 miles from the village of Kodiak and between two and three miles from the army cantonment. A skinny corporal from Headquarters Company, 37th Infantry, was the designated mail clerk continuing this prize duty assignment from the staging area at Camp Clatsop near Astoria, Oregon. He would wait for a messenger from the Navy to drive to the army to tell him mail was in, there not being any telephones at that time.

"Sir Corporal Mail Chief," as the clerk was lovingly called to his face because he brought the sought after "sugar" reports from girl friends and wives in "the states," took his assigned Dodge ¼-ton weapons-carrier (truck) to the navy and fetched the sacks of mail. Sometimes he went aboard the ship, signed for mail with the ship's purser, then waited for the sacks to be hoisted from the ship's hold by derrick and plopped on to the dock.

In the early day of the Army at the newly constructed "fort," there was little more than a battalion of the Federalized Calif-

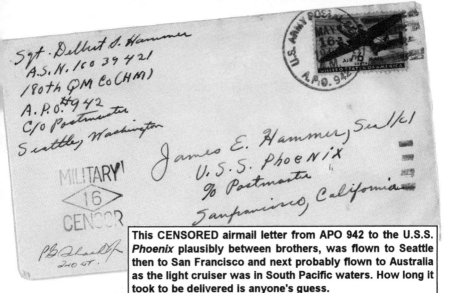

This CENSORED airmail letter from APO 942 to the U.S.S. *Phoenix* plausibly between brothers, was flown to Seattle then to San Francisco and next probably flown to Australia as the light cruiser was in South Pacific waters. How long it took to be delivered is anyone's guess.

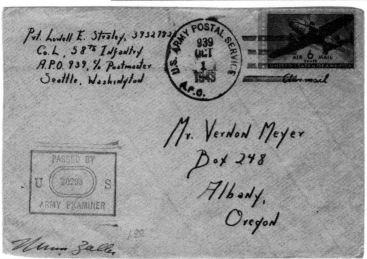

Letter from an infantryman at Dutch Harbor is classic format with CENSOR imprint, officer's signature. Soldier's serial number indicates he was probably drafted from the west coast.

Letters ready for mailing were submitted to units censor unsealed. After the censor finished his reading, the censor sealed the envelope. Sealed letters were not accepted by the units and were returned to the sender. When a BASE CENSOR selected letters at random for re-checking, the censor cut off the left end then resealed with imprinted cellophane tape. It was not unusual for a letter to bear two, even three CENSOR imprints.

Corporal Ray, of the Quartermaster Detachment at Fort Greely posted this airmail letter to Cleveland, Ohio on March 22, 1944. During this period the War Department insisted that APO numbers in the "dial" of the postmark be cut out for security reasons. Soldier was probably a draftee from the mid-west. The CENSOR impression is of the standard design used by unit commands. Somebody, someplace, had a list of the serial numbers of all those rubber stamps which were used in the Army world-wide.

ornia National Guard from San Francisco, the 250th Coast Artillery, Harbor Defense, and its medics. What could be called a "casual company," men of the Signal Corps, Quartermaster and Ordnance, were attached to a battalion of the 37th Infantry, also staged at Camp Clatsop, arrived in mid-July. The mail was not a burden on facilities and was handled from a small room in the post headquarters.

Soon the 215th Coast Artillery (anti-aircraft) Minnesota National Guard, arrived "in force." With the added load of mail coming in due to the increase of troops, the mail clerk's ¼-ton Dodge grew to a 1½-ton Chevy.

The 15 men in the Signal Corps Detachment,* who wanted to get mail to Seattle fast, learned, by the "network of rumors," to hand carry their letters to the bag that always hung on the gang-

*All Signal Corps men going to various posts in Alaska, except the ACS, during peace-time, were members of the parent unit, 8th Signal Service Company, Presidio of San Francisco. Eventually, a new unit, the 14th Signal Service Company, with headquarters at Fort Richardson, Anchorage, came into being and all of the men were automatically transferred into it. The ACS, 1st Signal Service Company, as mentioned earlier in this book, had been in Alaska under various unit designations since 1904.

This self-censored letter from a Coast Artillery officer bears what appears as a home-made leather CENSOR stamp. The postmark is from the Naval Air Station at Dutch Harbor.

plank leading to a ship in port at the Navy base, or anyone could do the same thing with ships tied up at one of the two docks in Kodiak.

(It was not a big deal to "take off" for the Navy, go fishing or go hunting in those days as the detachment did not at that time have any duty. But one could not go to town of Kodiak without first obtaining a pass from the unit commander.)

It was handy that ship's pursers traditionally accepted all mail deposited in the gang-plank sack which was by a small sign advising the ports-of-call the ship expected to visit. Mail deposited in those sacks was postmarked in Seattle and sent on its was a week or so later.

When too much "word-of mouth" leaked about this deluxe service and the gang-plank sack became overloaded by soldier's mail, complaints to the army quickly placed the navy's docks "off limits" thus the practice ground to a halt.

Once the war started (December 8, 1941), all mail was suddenly subject to censorship by unit commanders. (Civilian outgoing mail from the town post office was picked up and spot-checked by Army censors.) This lead to severe consternation in the ranks as this meant the lowest officer in the unit, frequently an unpopular officer in "line" outfits, was ordered to read all personal letters to make certain no "military secrets" were contained in them. Many of the men took the censorship personally and refused to send love letters knowing their officers would be

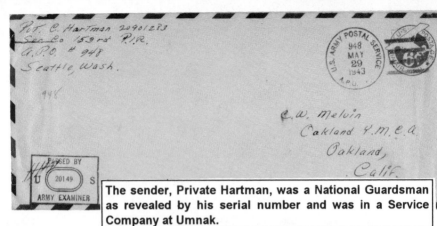

The sender, Private Hartman, was a National Guardsman as revealed by his serial number and was in a Service Company at Umnak.

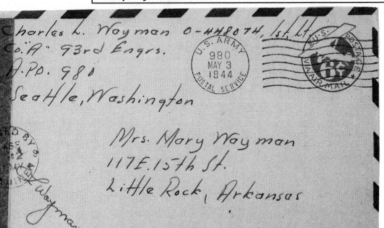

1st Lt. Wayman of the 93rd Engineers self-censored his letter to his wife then it was mailed at Adak's Air Force post office. All letters were subject to rechecking by ARMY EXAMINER.

Capt. Vowe, a coast artilleryman stationed at Dutch Harbor, sent this CENSORED piece, maybe a "get-well" card, to his friend in hospital at Vancouver, Washington. The letter is self-censored. Note missing APO number.

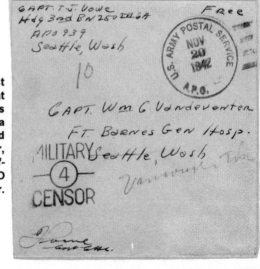

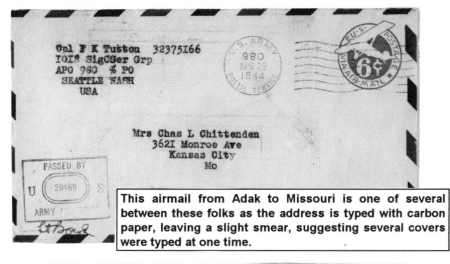

Cpl F K Tutton 32375166
IOIS SigCSer Grp
APO 980 % PO
SEATTLE WASH
USA

Mrs Chas L Chittenden
3621 Monroe Ave
Kansas City
Mo

PASSED BY
U 20468 S
ARMY

This airmail from Adak to Missouri is one of several between these folks as the address is typed with carbon paper, leaving a slight smear, suggesting several covers were typed at one time.

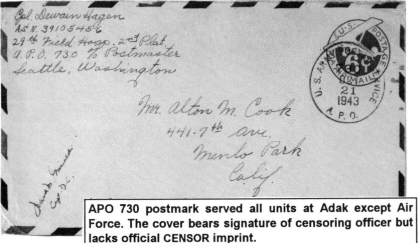

Cpl. Dewain Hagen
A.S.N. 39105456
29th Field Hosp. 2nd Plat.
A.P.O. 730 % Postmaster
Seattle, Washington

Mr. Alton M. Cook
441-7th Ave.
Menlo Park
Calif.

APO 730 postmark served all units at Adak except Air Force. The cover bears signature of censoring officer but lacks official CENSOR imprint.

reading their personal mail. In many units, the Signal Corps Detachment included, the Commanding Officer as-signed a high-ranking Sergeant to do the deed. The officer would merely sign all the fronts of the envelopes and hit the cover with a censor rubber stamp at he end of the day.

These were days before felt-tip pens had been invented as tools for blocking out writing therefore the censoring was done with a razor blade and Ohhhhh— never write on both sides of a sheet of paper!

Both pre-war, and later to cheat the unit censor, especially the Sergeant, from reading love letters, some mail still went to the

167

Sergeant Louis Aloe presents an interesting speculation as to what was his job? The DEML (Detached from Enlisted Men's List) indicate this regular army man from 3rd Service Command was on a special assignment of some kind. His letter from either Tanaga or Amchitka to Lt. Hartman at Adak was not subject to censorship as its destination was within the local district.

Lt. Hiram Hartman's letter on Oct. 10, 1943 from Amchitka was self-censored then rechecked by U.S. ARMY EXAMINER and resealed with imprinted cellophane tape before leaving for Pennsylvania.

naval base, on the sly, and was dropped in the gang-plank ship's sacks. This became more difficult when the Navy posted Marine Guards on the docks. But some of the Marines were friendly to the dungarees-dressed soldier and would carry the letter(s) to the mail sack as a courtesy. Letters were also slipped into the out-

APO 726 was as far west and still on U. S. real estate as it was possible to go – Attu. Pvt. Wayne Gentry sent a series of letters, mostly written on ships, on the way to Attu to a classmate "Lucious-Lou" Boise at Oregon State College. See remarks on pages 17-18.

From APO 942 to Seattle, Wash. The address was incomplete so the letter was marked "unclaimed" and returned.

going mail box of Siems-Drake Puget Sound civilian construction workers at the navy base. In the case of a few dozen men among thousands – having met some employees of the Alaska Steamship Company when their ships were in port and the men were in church on Sundays in Kodiak, these gentlemen willingly carried letters in their pockets to Seattle.

By the time more thousands of troops had arrived and a second cantonment was constructed and quickly filled, the Army Post Office at Fort Greely, and other places, had become a power house of efficiency. Now there were dozens of mail clerks and the

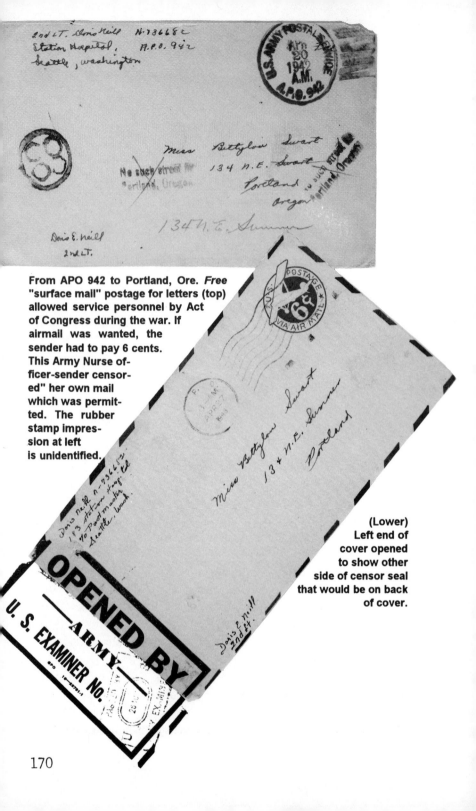

From APO 942 to Portland, Ore. *Free* "surface mail" postage for letters (top) allowed service personnel by Act of Congress during the war. If airmail was wanted, the sender had to pay 6 cents. This Army Nurse officer-sender censored" her own mail which was permitted. The rubber stamp impression at left is unidentified.

(Lower) Left end of cover opened to show other side of censor seal that would be on back of cover.

skinny Corporal was now a Staff Sergeant. The post office had its own building with heavy wire over its windows.

After airmail between the Naval Air Station and Seattle started, in addition to the loads from the ships, mail came at all hours of the day and night. It was not unusual for the phone in a barracks to ring say at 3 a.m. with a call to "come get your mail." There were never any complaints regardless of the hour.

When the author set up a photo lab in a skid-shack at the Army base having been appointed as Signal Corps Unit Photographer, there was no official equipment available. The only way to get equipment and technical supplies was to order directly from photo supply firms "stateside." This happened before censorship started and before the troop strength became so large that damage to parcels, already slowly beginning to creep into the mails, became really bad. (The traditional complaint that mother's home made cookies had to be eaten with a spoon was no lie!*) But

---

*About food. When the army invaded Alaska with the first troops, it was a peace-time army with peace-time rules. Each mess was headed by a Mess Sergeant most of whom were career soldier master-cooks and able administrators. (But there were obvious exceptions.) In "the states," these mess men bought food at the public wholesale market place. On foreign service, which included Alaska, foods came from the Post Quartermaster. Before the war, the quality and quantity was excellent. When the mess went on a war-time footing, the quality deteriorated. Gone were table settings and many other amenities. Cooks were on duty 24-hours a day to accommodate the 24-hour schedules. Meals for the outposts were prepared in the central messes and trucked to the gun positions. In the spring of 1942, ships were hauling in ammunitions and critical war material, not food. For weeks on end the mess was

Example of NAVY CENSOR at Dutch Harbor. War-time Navy postmarks did not reveal the location of the post office.

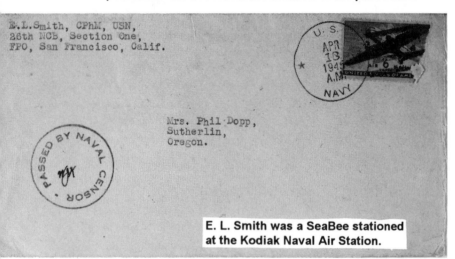

E. L. Smith was a SeaBee stationed at the Kodiak Naval Air Station.

trusting sensitive photographic equipment in the drop it, shove it, kick it, sit on it handling of much of the army package mail did not seem such a good idea.

But there was a solution: As most of the photo work in the Signal Corps Unit at that time was making snapshots of the men

mainly macaroni or boiled dry beans and fresh salmon, the fish caught by the KP's (kitchen police) in the nearby Buskin River by hand —pick the best ones.(See picture on p.10.) A few of the Signal Corps fellows had access to the "Ships Store" at the Navy base and brought back fresh pork sausage, steaks and other delights which were cooked in the skid-shack photo-lab at night on a plug-in hot plate. A number of the Signalmen considered the darkroom as a hangout and frequently used Webber's portable typewriter for writing letters.

(5¢ each), a "business" no less – common in the peace time army – why not rent a post office box in the Village of Kodiak? The rent was something like $1.50 a year? The fee was low but so was the army pay at $30 a month for a buck private which most men were.

In the peace-time army, many soldiers received their mail at off-post addresses. This was convenient for those at Fort Greely who knew about it, but the "line soldier" (infantry, artillery, engineers) didn't know of the town's post office availability. Even if they passed the post office when they were in town on weekends it was closed. (The Kodiak post office was not easily noticed for it was an old, gray, dilapidated building near Erskine's store and dock.)

The Kodiak postmaster was use to having enlisted men in uniform in his office because the Alaska Communications System (ACS) men lived in town in rented or owned houses. This handful of men got their mail at the Kodiak post office. When the war started and with it censorship, most of the ACS men lost their local post office accommodation for outgoing letters but kept their P.O. boxes for incoming mail as the service was faster. For the handful of us from Fort Greely with boxes, we just kept still about it. The author's box, No. 1135, was "active," that is the rent was paid on it, until he shipped out in May 1943. Nearly all of the equipment, including a new Royal portable typewriter, photo chemicals and other supplies, arrived at the Fort Greely photo lab by way of the town post office.

This civilian post office connection for military personnel was not unique to Kodiak. The author was in touch with a unit photog in the Signal Detachment at Anchorage and with another at Dutch Harbor (Unalaska). We all used local post offices for scrounging stuff between us and for buying photo supplies from "the states." Part of this was a safety measure because uniformed officer-censors (a few of whom seemed not to care), sometimes opened factory sealed boxes of film or photo sensitive paper thereby ruining it.

The official mail clerks, such as the Staff Sergeant at Fort Greely, had a job of great significance and trust. When the responsibility became ever bigger, he kept right on doing his work but a new 2nd Lt., recently from Officers Candidate School, was designated Postal Officer. There was need for an officer as the volume of official mail was large and most of it was "registered."

The registry of mail is a totally different ball game as the handling of every single piece of mail must be signed for at every step along the way from deposit with the post office until final delivery. To a lesser extent, "insured" parcel post must also be signed for. For some military destinations, insurance service was not available. As we shall see, there was always risk of non-delivery of uninsured parcels that had been mis-dispatched by the a post office in "the states."

The assignment of A.P.O. numbers to every army base world wide, was a great challenge to some of the civil service mail clerks in "the states." It was mandatory that mail be properly directed. In the Aleutians, a letter addressed to APO 944, Fort Randall at the secret air base at Cold Bay, but shoved into the wrong case in Seattle marked APO 942, would see the letter turn up at Fort Richardson in Anchorage over a thousand miles away. One of many of such mis-direction incidents was witnessed at Woman's Bay. During the unloading of a ship's mail, a box plainly addressed to the Post Exchange at Fort Mears was found but was never reshipped to Fort Mears—its contents were consumed where discovered. It had been shipped by the Hershey Chocolate Company.

Being a mail clerk in an individual outfit was considered very good duty especially in the Regular Army. Many of these men were quite sharp for they had to abide by all the postal regulations. But others were the goof-offs of the unit, primarily draftees, who didn't seem to fit other assignments – and this was sad.

As years spent in the military counted with a "point" preference in post-war jobs with the U. S. Post Office Department, thousands of former service men and women applied for and received appointments with the Post Office. Many of them learned basic mail-handling skills serving the APO system.

OS2U-3 Kingfisher scout – observation plane.

Chapter 21
OS2U –Kingfisher Patrols

As generally held in the gaze of recollection, the Kingfisher airplane has been most commonly thought of as one of those little pigeon scout planes that were thrust into the air from catapults on battleships and cruisers. These seaplanes indeed had that role.

Fletcher Sanders, now retired from the Navy, was a torpedoman whose job was to launch and retrieve Kingfishers. He wrote that nearly all of his war years had been spent on this duty on his "favorite ship" the U.S.S. *Richmond*. He recalled the unexpected baptism he got during the Battle of the Komondorski Islands when the cruiser, about the launch a Kingfisher, took a near-miss of a Japanese shell that splashed the ship and the Kingfisher mission was scrubbed.

With the Kingfishers, the mechanics at the operating bases could exchange the pontoons for a set of wheels or the other way around. The pilots were checked out in both land and water operations. The flight characteristics were considerably different between the two versions due to drag when fit with the floats.

There were three VS (observation - scouting) squadrons in war-time Alaska. These were operated from Adak, Dutch Harbor, and Kodiak.

Shuttered spotlight became "blinker" for sending messages by Morse code between ships at sea. Had been developed in Navy long before radio but was used in WW-II during radio-silence periods.

The Adak unit (VS-56) was unique as it not only had King-fishers but SBD Douglas Dauntless Dive-bombers. The thinking seems to have been if the Japanese brought in ships for another operation, as indeed they did for the evacuation of Kiska, the SBD's would be considerably more effective than the Kingfishers in the latter's very limited role as a dive-bomber. With the Kiska evacuation being carried out in the fog and the Americans totally unaware of it, the SBD flyers never got a chance to show their stuff.

The VS squadron at Dutch Harbor (VS-49) was primarily with floats due to the limited availability of airstrips along their scouting routes. The Kodiak unit (VS-70) also worked with floats but used wheels when on special search missions such as for downed aircraft. One such mission was a search in the Anchorage - Cordova area. The 90 - 100 knots cruising speed was excellent for being effective in search operations.

The Kodiak squadron had a detachment operating out of Cold Bay on wheels.

James W. Spencer, an OS2U-3 pilot operating out of Kodiak, wrote that the Kingfisher carried one 100 pound fragmentation bomb on each wing on patrols in the seaplane configuration. But on the flight to participate in the scout-and-sink of the *I-180*, they

Kingfisher-Eye View of Alaska's Beauty

A number of the pilots had small cameras and regularly made snapshots from their aircraft. As there was a spare bathroom in one of the quarters, they set up a darkroom where they processed and printed their own pictures. The unit censor, the Air Combat Intelligence Officer, approved photographs of people and those without military significance.

used land planes with a 350-pound depth charge under each wing quipping "maybe the depth charges were a bit much for the seaplanes."

The stormy ocean southwest of Kodiak seemed an unlikely place for enemy action as late as April of 1944 but it occurred. There had been no reports of Japanese submarines prowling into the waters off Alaska since the battles in the Aleutians in 1942-1943 but that situation suddenly changed.

A two-ship convoy of freighters, S.S. *Frank G. Drum* and S.S. *Greenup,* were southwest of Kodiak. For their protection, two destroyer-escorts, the *Gilmore* and the *Edward C. Daly* were nearby. At 2230, *Gilmore* came alive with a RADAR blip showing a surface contact 4 miles distance. The escort turned in the blip's direction to intercept and 5 minutes later, now just 2 miles away, challenged with blinker. Instead of replying, the RADAR contact disappeared. *Gilmore's* crew was ordered to battle stations and a deadly game of cat-and-mouse began. It lasted 2 hours and 37 minutes.

The target was presumed to be a Japanese submarine on a reconnaissance mission to see what the U.S. Navy was doing.

177

(Top) Kingfisher on floats lands at Cold Bay to deliver mail. (Lower) Wheeled version at Cold Bay following engine checkup. Mechanic on ground hand-rotates prop before pilot hits starter.

When detected, she had been caught on the surface recharging her batteries.

Gilmore attacked several times with patterns of Mark 10 then Mark 6 projectiles while *Daly* encoded a message to Alaska Sea Frontier Command that a contact had been made.

At the Naval Air Station on Kodiak, four Kingfishers with wheels, instead of floats, were fitted with 350 pound depth charges and readied for a search and destroy mission. It would be about a 2 hour flight to the site and the weather was the usual putrid. The four pilots assigned were Lt. Cdr Robert E. Ellis, leader; Lt. Ray Compton; Lt(jg) Peter Klein and Ensign James W. Spencer USNR.

At sea, the *Gilmore's* patterns had brought forth a tremendous underwater explosion from a depth of about 280 feet

– at least 20 feet below the sub's presumed "safe" dive limit. A little later an oil slick appeared but seeing this was nearly impossible in the inky night.

The *I-180* incident was one of the few during the Pacific War where wheel-fitted Kingfisher observation planes had been scrambled for a stated offensive action against the Japanese. The pilot shown, Ens. James W. Spencer, was on the mission but shown here while on a routine patrol out of Kodiak.

The Kingfishers arrived just at dawn. Although there was no sign of a ship (*Gilmore* was hidden in the fog), the pilots saw and reported a huge oil slick about one mile square and so thick to prevent white caps breaking in a 35 knot wind. The location was plotted at 55°10' N - 155° 40' W. This was about 50 miles from tiny Chirikof Island. The *Gilmore* had apparently sunk whatever was down there. As there was no need to waste their ordnance, the OS2U's returned to Kodiak.

The Action Report of April 26, 1944 rated the incident as "probable kill." Positive confirmation was made after the war when the Japanese acknowledged it was their *I-180* that had been lost that night.

*   *   *

The observation squadrons had their losses just as did the bomber and fighter squadrons. One of the Kingfishers ran out of luck on landing at Kodiak NAS and ended in the bay. The pilot was rescued but the airplane did not fare so well.

A more serious incident occurred with one of the SBD's that had

Naval Air Station – Kodiak.
Woman's Bay (left) at edge of Old
Woman's Mountain. Next mountain
is Mt. Barometer an indictor of the
weather. If one could see Mt. Barometer, it was about to rain. If one
could not see it, it was raining. See
photo on page 8.
(Inset) Wheeled OS2U ran out of
runway, rolled into the bay. Pilot was
saved but his airplane was not.

been at Kodiak for routine maintenance. When ready for the return, Lt
(jg) Ralph Hannula volunteered to ferry it back to VS-56 at Adak. He
did the usual island-to-island hopping but on the last leg, he and his
airplane simply disappeared. Although searches were made, neithert
he nor any of his airplane was ever found.

All three Kingfisher squadrons at the Alaska bases were pulled
back to the states in December 1944. Those from down the chain
island-jumped to Kodiak then went either to Yakutat directly or there
by way of Elmendorf. The next stop was to Annette Island near Sitka
then to one of two RCAF bases on Vancouver Island. The final hop
was to Sand Point NAS on Lake Washington in Seattle.

Japanesse scout-observation "ALF" plane, from cruiser *Abukuma,* landed at Kiska.

Chapter 21
How the Japanese Did It
Their Aleutian Campaign*

The Japanese plans for the occupation of selected islands in the Western Aleutians, Territory of Alaska, U.S.A. was for the purpose of blocking a United States advance against the Japanese home islands from the north.

The Commander of the 1st Destroyer Squadron and his staff learned of this plan late in April 1942. The original intention was to occupy Adak, Kiska and Attu but as a result of the Battle of Midway, the plan for Adak was cancelled and that force was used to occupy Attu. There was also a reconnaissance of Amchitka. Afterwards, the 1st Destroyer Squadron was active in supply and support of the Aleutians mostly during summer months because of bad weather in winter.

---

*This chapter is based on USSBS No. 367 *Aleutian Campaign : Operations of the Japanese First Destroyer Squadron.*

Compilation of Data on Chart Based on
Interrogation NAV No. 73
United States Strategic Bombing Survey No. 367
Interviews of of Key Japanese Naval Officers
by
Captain James S. Russell, USN

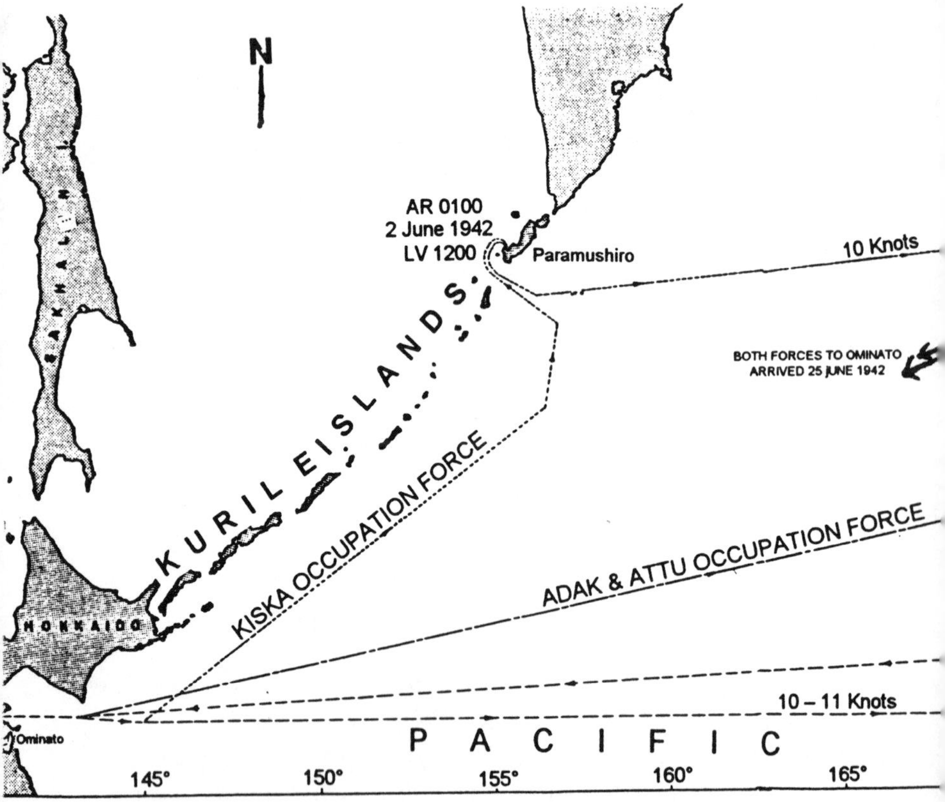

N

AR 0100
2 June 1942
LV 1200   Paramushiro

10 Knots

BOTH FORCES TO OMINATO
ARRIVED 25 JUNE 1942

KURIL EISLANDS

KISKA OCCUPATION FORCE

ADAK & ATTU OCCUPATION FORCE

HONKAIDO

Ominato

10 – 11 Knots

P A C I F I C

145°   150°   155°   160°   165°

MOVEMENT OF JAPANESE FORCES
ALEUTIAN CAMPAIGN 1942
Dates and Times are TOKYO TIME MINUS 9

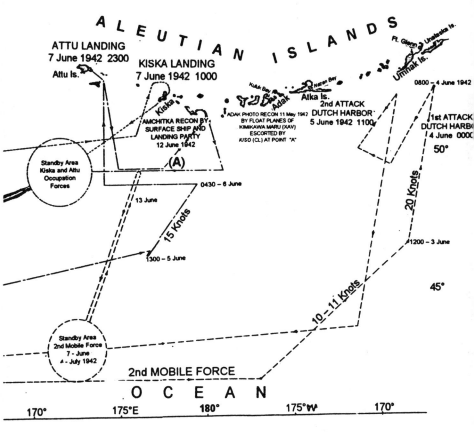

ALEUTIAN ISLANDS

ATTU LANDING
7 June 1942 2300

Attu Is.

KISKA LANDING
7 June 1942 1000

Kiska

Kuluk Bay

Adak

Atka Is.

Nazan Bay

Ft. Glenn Unalaska Is.

Umnak Is.

0800 – 4 June 1942

AMCHITKA RECON BY
SURFACE SHIP AND
LANDING PARTY
12 June 1942

ADAK PHOTO RECON 11 May 1942
BY FLOAT PLANES OF
KIMIKAWA MARU (XAV)
ESCORTED BY
KISO (CL) AT POINT "A"

2nd ATTACK
DUTCH HARBOR
5 June 1942 1100

2nd ATTACK
DUTCH HARBO
4 June 0000

(A)

Standby Area
Kiska and Attu
Occupation
Forces

0430 – 6 June

50°

13 June

15 Knots

20 Knots

1300 – 5 June

1200 – 3 June

45°

10 – 11 Knots

Standby Area
2nd Mobile Force
7 - June
4 - July 1942

2nd MOBILE FORCE

O C E A N

170°   175°E   180°   175°W   170°

RECON BY SUBMARINES
I-25 (Kodiak) I-26 (Str of Juan d'Fuca)

183

Japanese aircraft carrier *Ryujo*.

隼鷹艦爆隊ダッチハーバー爆撃略図

昭和17年6月5日 （編集部作成）

ベーリング海

ダッチハーバー

三浦機退路

A

阿部機退路

P40九機と交戦

ウムナク島

進入路

X

ウナラカス島

B

集合点

ウムナク水道

阿部機よりおくれて集合点に
達した三浦機他七機は　敵戦
闘機と交戦

Map with tracks of flight of attackers on third air raid on Dutch Harbor. Col.
Abe turned to left at point "A" to return to carrier. He was intercepted at "X"
by nine P-40 fighters from secret base on Umnak. Pilot Miura and 7 Japanese
planes turned to right at "A" for flight back to carrier, would parallel Abe. Of
the 11 attackers on this raid, 2 were shot down as well as 2 scouts from
cruisers by P-40's. Abe's plane was damaged at "B" became hard to fly. He
was late getting to carrier. His shipmates thought he was down. Abe wrote,
"It was a beautiful day in May but the task was hard and regretable work –
painful memory due to loss of life."

This activity ended in the Battle of the Komondorski Islands on 27 March 1943 (Tokyo time) when a convoy to Attu was being escorted in force by the 5th Fleet. This action stopped further supply by surface craft except for one or two dashes to Attu by destroyers. Later efforts was made to resupply using submarines. When Attu was retaken by the United States, the 1st Destroyer Squadron was assigned to evacuate the Kiska garrison. The second attempt was successful under heavy fog between 1340 and 1435 on 29 July (Tokyo time and date).

Interrogation of Vice Admiral Sentaro Omori, IJN, Commander of 1st Destroyer Squadron operating from flagship light cruiser *Abukuma* October 1940 to October 1942. Omori was relieved by Rear Admiral T. Mori in Nov. 1942 through June 1943. Admiral M. Kimura was commander afterward.

Q.: "What was the date of the planning for occupation of Aleutians and when did Admiral Omori first know of it"? Ans.: "About May 1942."

The plan was to originally go directly and occupy Adak then on to occupy Attu. The force was *ABUKUMA*, with 21st Destroyer Div, one battalion of Army troops on *Kinugasa Maru*; seaplane tender *Kimikawa* escorted by probably 2 destroyers and the mine layer *Kogane Maru*. The army troops were commanded by Major Hozumi.

This was the plan but what took place was slightly different.

The Adak landing force left Japan and went to about 44° N - 178° W when word was flashed about the defeat at Midway. Because Midway was a decisive battle, the Combined Chiefs ordered that the occupation of Aleutians be cancelled. The force in the northern waters proceeded toward Adak about 60 miles then reversed course to rendezvous with 1st Fleet. After about 120 miles and sending *Kogane Maru* back to Japan, new orderes directed to continue the Aleutian occupation plans. When the force was back to about 45° North, orders were received to occupy Attu and not Adak with the forces then in the convoy but sending *Kimikawa Maru* to Kiska to help with the Kiska occupying force then enroute from another direction. The remaining force, the *Abukuma*, 21st Destroyer Div (*Nenchi, Hatsuharu, Hatsushimo, Wakaba*) and *Kinugasa Maru* arrived in Holtz Bay, Attu on 11 June and started the landing one hour before sunrise.

Occupation of Attu and Kiska

From Holtz Bay the troops moved overland to Chgichagof Harbor arriving from the landward side. The party was confused with directions and crossed the island to Massacre Bay before going to Chgichagof Harbor. When

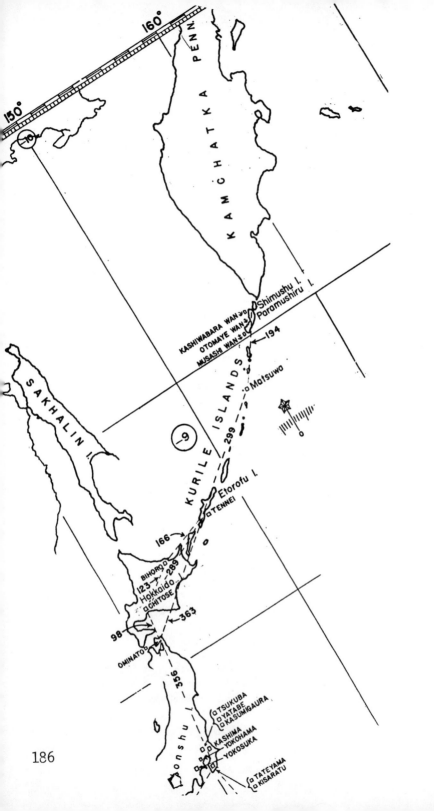

160°

150°

KAMCHATKA PENN.

SAKHALIN I.

Shimushu I.
Paramushiru I.
KASHIWABARA WAN
OTOMAYE WAN
MUSASH WAN
194

Matsuwo

KURILE ISLANDS

299

9

Etorofu I.
TENNEI

166

BIHORO
289
123
Hokkaido
CHITOSE

363

98
OMINATO

356

Honshu

TSUKUBA
YATABE
KASUMIGAURA

KASHIMA
YOKOHAMA
YOKOSUKA

TATEYAMA
KISARATU

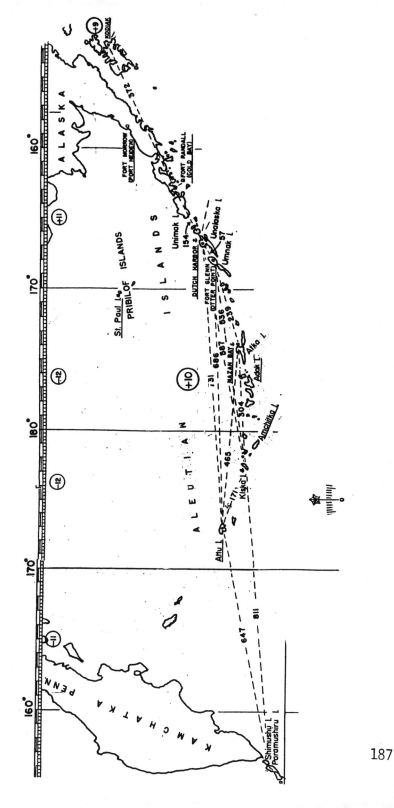

the arrived there they found only about 40 natives and 2 Americans. The *Kinugasa Maru* entered the harbor about noon and unloaded supplies remaining there until about 13 June while the 1st destroyer Div. patrolled off shore.

The destroyers also conducted a reconnaissance of the Semichi Islands to see if they were suitable for an airfield, then departed on 13 June to Amchitka to look for suitability for building airfield. Slightly before sunrise, the *Nenohi* put a landing party ashore at Constantine Harbor while aircraft from *Abukuma* explored Amchitka by air. The *Abukuma* cruised along the north side to look at the shoreline. This survey took about 3 hours then the force met off the southeast end of the island at which time an American plane was seen. The weather was bad and no action took place by either side.

The force then retires to an area about 49° 20' N - 171° 40' E where the 21st Destroyer Div. was ordered to Kiska. Meanwhile light cruiser *Kiso* joined *Abukuma* at rendezvous. The 6th Destroyer Div consisting of *Akatsuki, Hibiki, Inazuma, Ikazuchi* were attached to the Kiska Occupation Force. About the 19th, *Hibiki,* having been damaged by American bombs at Kiska was ordered to Japan.

The *Abukuma* returned to Ominato, Japan about 25th June and left again on the 30th in company with Carrier Div. 4 and 5, Cruiser Div 5. and battle Cruiser Div. 3. The purpose was to support the Kiska operation. The carriers cruised to an area centered about 43° N - 173° E to be in position to intercept any American forces that might come up from Midway to interfere with the Kiska landing.

While the carrier force was standing by beginning the 3rd or 4th of July, the 18th Destroyer Div. *Kasumi, Arare, Shiranuhi*) that had sailed from Japan, was operating in the Kiska area. The ships were attacked by an American submarine on the 5th. *Arare* was sunk. The others were significantly damaged thus cruiser *Abukuma* proceeded to Kiska to help and stayed until 12th or 13th of July.

On 5 July *Nenohi* was sunk by submarine off Agattu Island. Only 30 survivors, all enlisted personnel, reached Agattu. About 12th or 13th July *Abukuma* left Kiska for Yokosuka, then returned to Ominato by the end of July. From that time to end of October, the cruiser *Abukuma* was command ship for destroyers going to Aleutians but she did not go there herself operating between Kataoka and Kakumabetsu, Paramushiro and Ominato.

On 20th Oct, *Abukuma, Kiso* and *Tama* carried 900 troops, commanded by Lt. Col. Yonekawa, to Attu escorted by 2 destroyers. The destroyers were from 21st Destroyer Div. and probably were the *Hatsushimo* and *Wakaba*. The troops replaced the earlier complement which had been moved to Kiska. With the evacuation of Attu's men to Kiska, Attu had been left with only a small naval radio unit between about the end of August and 20th of October.

About the middle of October destroyers *Oboro* and *Hatsuharu* were carrying supplies to Kiska and near the north end of Kiska, the *Hatsuharu* was heavily damaged by air attack. There were additional air attacks by the Americans but Admiral Omori said he did not know the details..

Hibiki DD

Japanese Ships in the Western Aleutians
This list may not be complete
CV aircraft carrier CA Heavy cruiser CL Light cruiser DD Destroyer

Chiyoda (CV)   11,190T (1938)

Maya (CA)	11,350T (1932)		*Nenohi* (DD)	1,490T (1933)
Nachi (CA)	10,940T (1928)		*Oboro* (DD)*	1,680T (1931)
Abukuma (CL)	5,170T (1925)		*Samidare*(DD)	1,685T (1937)
Kiso (CL)	5,100T (1921)		*Shimakase* (DD)	2,567T (1943)
Tama (CL)	5,100T (1921)		*Shiokaze* (DD	1,215T (1921)

Kimikawa Maru (tender) 6,937T (1938)

Shiranuhi (DD)   2,033T (1939)
Usugumo (DD)   1,680T (1928)

Magane Maru (minelayer)

Wakaba (DD)   1,490T (1934)
Yugumo (DD)   2,077T (-----)

Akatsuki (DD)	1,680T (1932		
Akigumo (DD)	2,077T (1941)	*Akagane Maru* (transport
Arare (DD)	1,961T (1939)	*Awata Maru* (transport)
Asagumo (DD)	1,961T (1938)	*Asaka Maru* (transport)
Hatsushimo (DD	1,490T (1934)	*Kano Maru* (transport)
Hatsuharu (DD)	1,490T (1933)	*Kinugasa Maru* (transport)
Hibiki (DD)	1,680T (1933)	*Nissan Maru* (transport)
Hokaze (D)	1,215T (1920)	*Nojima Maru* (transport)
Ikaduchi (DD)	1,680T (1932)	*Sakito Maru* (transport)
Inadzuma (DD)	1,680T (1932)	*Sanko Maru* (transport)
Kasumi (DD)	1,961T (1939)	
Kazagumo (DD	2,077T (1942)	*Kunajiri* (picket boat)
Naganami (DD)	2,077T (1942)	

Teiyo Marul (tanker)

Maya CA

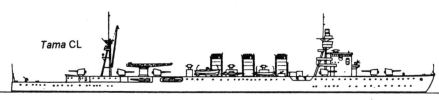
Tama CL

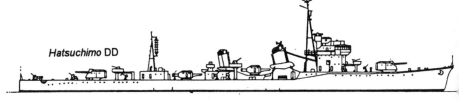
Hatsuchimo DD

189

On arrival at Attu evening of 22-23 October, the men and cargoes were discharged with great haste so the ships could be at a safe distance west of Attu to avoid any attacks by the Americans from Dutch Harbor and Amchitka expected the next morning. The troops were all infantry and brought with them about 30 days of food and ammunition. About 6 Nov., the ships went back to Ominato and Admiral Omori was relieved by Admiral Mori.

During the Attu and Kiska occupation, the Japanese admiral said cruiser *Abukuma* was never under attack.

The approach routes to get into Kiska Harbor was to approach from the western end of the island and north around Kiska to the harbor. Some ships went straight from Paramushiro to a point due south of Kiska then turned for the run straight in. These approaches were considered the best because of great danger of air or submarine attacks.

This ended the interrogation with Admiral Omorti.

* * *

Captain James S. Russell, USA, then talked with Captain Rokuki Arichika, IJN, who was Chief of Staff to Commander 1st Destroyer Squadron from December 1941 until November 1943

Q.: "When did you first learn of the plan to occupy the Aleutian Islands"? Ans.: "At the end of April."

Q.: "What was the purpose of the Aleutian Operations"? A.: "The Aleutian Operations were a defensive measure against possible American attack coming from the North."

> **Captain Arichika pointed out that the operation was not a success because of failure to make proper preparations. The major omission was failure to plan for building airfields.**

Captain Archika's experiences were largely in summer due to "terrific winter weather." He was part of the Attu invasion and later was involved in transport and escort operations.

The battalion of Army troops, known as the *Hokkaido Daitai,* was on the 7,000 to 8,000 ton 15-knot *Kinugasa Maru* that left Ominato about 29th of May and went to about 44° N - 178° W where it arrived about 5th June then started directly toward Adak. When the bad news of the Battle of Midway arrived, the 1st Destroyer Div. was ordered to join the Midway force therefore the destroyers reversed course. In less than one hour that order was superseded with the force directed to proceed to Attu. The Adak occupation plan was abandoned. *Abukuma, Kinugasa Maru, Wakaba, Hatsushimo* and *Nenohi* went to Attu, the force arriving there about 2100 or 2200 on 7 June. Troops were landed at 2300. At first there was fear the landings had been made in the wrong place but at 0300 on 8 June a report came that the landing was successful.

> **"I believe the dates Admiral Omori gave are in error [but] the dates I [Capt. Arichika] have given are correct."**

Captain Arickika said he recalls the dates from the reports of the Kiska landings which were nearly simultaneously but a little earlier.

Captain Russell asked Captain Arichika what he knew about Captain Ito's unit of 6 Mavis flying boats at Attu. He replied he saw them but at Kiska. He said that Chichagof Harbor was not used for the initial landing because the harbor was too narrow and shallow. The original plan was to by-pass Chichagof and go to Holtz Bay but the Army put troops ashore at Holtz Bay and made the mistake of going south across the island to Massacre Bay intending on going east to Chichagof. This caused a delay in the operations.

The cruiser *Abukuma* left the entrance of Holtz Bay and went to the entrance of Chichagof Harbor where by about 0700 next day, the Army's troops could be seen coming down the mountains to Chichagof Harbor. He said that until 10 June, ships from 1st Destroyer Squadron patrolled around Attu then left for Amchitka. They went into Constantine Harbor on or about 12 June. The reconnaissance at Amchitka was to investigate the possibility of building an airfield there.

The ships on the Amchitka mission were *Abukuma, Wakaba,* and one other destroyer. The shore party was all from *Wakaba*. While so occupied, an American plane was reported by one of the ships but was not sighted. It was believed the plane was patrolling between Amchitka and Kiska. As there was risk the airplane had spotted the survey parts and the ships, orders from *Abukuma* were rushed to the landed party to hurry back to for a speedy departure. The ships fled at 20 knots hoping to avoid detection. The ships went to the standby area about 200 miles south of Kiska and stayed about 3 or 4 days.

The American airplane had been sighted about 6 or 7 o'clock in the morning. The offshore standby at distance of about 200 miles was to be out of sight of the American bombers. The force also wanted to ascertain the results of the bombing and what further developments might ensue before going back to Japan. It was believed the bombers were B-17s. The destroyer *Hibiki* was bombed and damaged probably between 13 and 15 of June. *Kiso,* undamaged, also at Kiska, left for the standby area. The *Hibiki* was towed by *Akatsuki* to Ominato and arrived there about 26 or 27 June.

While in the standby area from which regular patrols around the Aleutians, when weather (heavy fog) permitted, were carried out, regular radio communications with Kiska were maintained. The Japanese ships went for their look sees under cover of fog and when the sun came out, scooted back into the fog to avoid being bombed.

At the end of June, the force returned to Ominato for a few days then went back to the Aleutians. Standing by in waters well south of Attu was a carrier group. The *Chiyoda* went to Kiska covered by destroyers *Kasumi, Arare, Shiranuhi,* the destroyers stationed themselves north of Little Kiska Island at 0300 5 July. They were promptly attacked by an American submarine.

The first torpedo sank the *Arare,* which was closest to the submarine from a range estimated at 1,000 meters. A second torpedo smashed *Kasumi* just forward of the bridge and almost broke off her bow which dropped to about 30 degrees below horizontal. The third torpedo missed *Shiranuhi*, farthest from the attacker but the 4th torpedo hit *Shiranuhi* amidships and severed the hull plating and the bottom to that the damaged destroyer was held together only by her main deck and centerline structure.

Captain Arichika exclaimed to Admiral Russell during the interrogation, "This was a skillful attack by the American submarine and was admirably executed." With the wreckage now littering Kiska harbor, the *Abunka* and *Wakaba* and one other destroyer braved the risks of being seen and bombed and went to Kiska to help with the salvage of the two broken destroyers.

On the same day, 5 July, while *Nenohi* was escorting a tanker, the tanker was attacked by a submarine. *Nenohi* responded by attacking the submarine and sank it off Chichagof Harbor. This sinking was confirmed by viewing debris and oil slick. Regrettably, later in the day, *Nenohi* was sunk while making 6 knots close in to Agattu. She was struck from abaft the starboard beam by one submarine torpedo. *Nenohi* capsized within 2 minutes and sank within 5 minutes. One of her boats came adrift as she went down and into this scrambled 20 of her crew (all that were apparently saved) and made for Agattu Island.

* * *

In returning to the narrative about the severe damage to *Kasumi*, the hull was broken and her bow hung low so she would not move. A technician from Yokosuka Navy Yard was called into conference to survey the damage to help determine if the bow should be cut off or if the ship should be brought back to Japan as it was. Captain Arichika indicated he thought the bow was cut off then the remains were towed back to Japan.

The *Shiranuhi's* hull was ruptured on both sides but was held together just with the deck and the centerline structure. This break was abaft the forward stack. Engineers put patches on the hull at Kiska then she was towed back to Maizuru. The *Kasumi* and the *Shiranuhi* returned there about the same time, around the end of July or early August. They stopped at Paramushiro on the way.

The *Abukuma, Wakaba* and *Ikazushi* left Kiska about the 10th of July for Yokosuka and got in about the 16th or 17th. These ships went into repair dock for overhaul. The conditions at Kiska were reported to the *GUNREIBU* (Naval General Staff) in Tokyo. On 2 August these ships prepared to get underway from Ominato and sailed on the 3rd. After an uneventful cruise, they came in at Ominato on the 5th.

There were plans for training exercises including firing of torpedoes but on the 8th of August, 5 American cruisers and some destroyers did a bombardment against Kiska. The training mission was cancelled and the ships left for Kiska the night of the 8th and went into Paramushiro on the 10th or 11th of August. The *Kiso*, which was also at Ominato went along to Paramushiro where the Fifth Fleet rendezvoused and readied for a voyage to Kiska. Word was received from Kiska that the American naval force had stopped the cannonade and departed therefore the Fifth Fleet did not sortie.

The Fifth Fleet at that time was organized in this manner:

Nachi (Fleet flag), *Kiso, Tama*
1st Destroyer Div. *Shiokaze, Hokaze*
1st Destroyer Squadron. *Abukuma* (Squadron flag)
21st Destroyer Div. *Wakaba, Hatsushimo, Hatsuharu*
6th Destroyer Div. *Ikazuchi, Inazuma*
(Independent) *Usugumo*
Tanker *Teiyo Maru*
(The tanker and 1st Destroyer Div were normally under the Commandant, Ominato but joined the Fleet during sorties.)

Regarding the American naval bombardment of Kiska, the only ships in harbor were two grounded transports that were earlier damaged by air attacks. These were the *Nojima Maru* and *Kano Maru*. Also the *Nissan Maru* which had been previously sunk but whose bridge and mast still stuck above the water. The *Kasumi* and the *Shiranuhi* might have been present. Also, there were 5 midget two-man submarines there. However, there were no cruisers or battleships or destroyers, The seaplane tender *Kimikawa Maru* may also have been there. There was no damage to any of these ships in the harbor. The damage was mostly to warehouses on shore. Some airplanes were destroyed but the number was not known. Three men were acknowledged as killed. There were some presumed wounded but no numbers were given. The Chief of Staff of the Fifth Fleet, Rear Admiral Tasaku Nakazawa, who had arrived by destroyer, was at Kiska during the bombardment.

From the time the Fifth Fleet arrived at Paramushiro until February of he next year, there were "absolutely no offensive operations" carried out by the Fifth Fleet as such. There were training exercises while the destroyers and the *Kiso* made transport runs to Attu and to Kiska. These were exciting because in order to avoid detection by American planes, the ships had to run in during the night, rush with unloading cargo then get clear of the harbor before daylight.

The American occupation of Adak was like a "thorn in the side." Intelligence reports were received that the Americans were building airfields there very rapidly.

> The Americans were building an airfield at Adak very rapidly and this worried us because we realized that we would soon be subjected to additional land-based bombing attacks.

The exact date the Japanese learned of the American occupation of Adak was not recalled but reports came in from reconnaissance flights probably about the first of October. The Japanese said they were "surprised at the speed with which the building of the airbase progressed."

The Japanese had planned to occupy the Semichi Islands and to construct airfields there but the lack of personnel and time to make the occupation, therefore the Japanese held only Attu, Agattu and Kiska.

Method for Running Supplies Into Kiska and Attu

Transport operations were very difficult to carry out because to avoid detection by American aircraft during daylight hours, the Japanese had to take advantage of storms and fog. Planning runs to meet the bad weather was a challenge for the meteorologists but had to be done.

Three, 17-knot transports were employed for the speed runs. These were the *Asaka Maru, Sakito Maru, Awata Maru* as well as light cruisers and even destroyers. A scouting radius of 600 miles from Adak and Amchitka was considered as it was presumed that American planes would search a 15 degree sector. When a transport arrived at the 600 mile radius, a dash in to the harbor was made using radio intelligence of the planes airborne to choose an uncovered sector of approach or, to follow in through a sector behind a plane which was scouting there. The route away was also chosen on radio messages of the air scouting in progress choosing the sector which was not covered by air, or following the outbound track of a search airplane.

Radio intelligence of the search plane call signs was an aid in determining the uncovered sectors also, RADAR reports from Kiska assisted with this function. It was never possible for the Japanese to break down the aircraft code successfully. The various approaches to Kiska were labeled "A," "B," "C" and so on and from intelligence plotted on the *Abukuma*, a track for running into Kiska was determined and given to the ships on the mission. This system was very successful.

During one of the transport operations, the *Akagane Maru* was sunk by shelling by an American cruiser. The ship was at 53° 20' N - 171° E and a picket boat, the *Kunajiri,* which heard the sounds of gunfire was only about 25,000-26,000 meters to the west. When this attack happened, cruiser *Kiso* and *Sakito Maru* were about 200 miles to the north. A seaplane tender reported the American cruisers to be steaming east after the sinking. If *Kiso* and *Sakito Maru* had continued toward Kiska they would have been intercepted by the American cruisers therefore they turned away.

At this same time, *Abukuma* and the *Awata Maru* were on their way to Kiska at about 56° 20' - 171° 30' E. *Abukuma* and the *Asaka Maru* with a destroyer, continued on and went to Kiska.

The *Abukuma* and the one destroyer escorted the *Asaka Maru* to a point about 120 miles north of Kiska then the transport went on in to Kiska alone. The escorts reversed course and set for Paramushiro because of the great number of American planes in the vicinity. During 21st of February, *Abukuma* and her destroyer took the most northerly course possible for the return voyage. They swung up to about 59° N reaching the northern point on the night of the 21nd, then proceeded south between Bering Island and the Gulf of Kamchatka to Paramushiro arriving there about the 24th or 25th. (This was a long way out of the way following a philosophy of "better be safe than sorry" due to increasing distances being flown by American patrols.)

194

Lt. Bill Macbeth at Japanese anti-aircraft gun in Chichagof - Holtz area of Attu 1944. The grass on this alluvial shelf was so tall and husky it was difficult to walk through.

When a cargo ship arrived at Kiska, the garrison turned out in great numbers to stevedore the vessel due to the urgent need for its goods and immense risk of being caught by American bombers. The merchantman *Awata Maru* was in Kiska Harbor only about one hour for unloading then moved right out to sea and returned directly to Yokosuka by a southern route.

Because of the sinking of *Akagane Maru* by American naval guns, a change in transport plans were mandated. Transports would no longer be sent one or two at a time but would, starting in March, be in convoys. The entire Fifth Fleet consisting of the 1st Destroyer Squadron, the *Nachi, Maya* and Tama (*Kiso* was believed to be in Maizuru at that time). Transports *Asaka Maru* and *Sakito Maru* went to Attu where they arrived safely in March.

The 1st Destroyer Div. at this time consisted of:

Abukuma (flag ship), *Wakaba, Hatsuharu, Hatsushimo, Inazuma, Ikazuchi, Usugumo.* During the night the larger vessels (*Nachi, Maya, Tama*) with *Inazuma* and *Ikazuchi* patrolled about 20 miles off shore north of Attu. The *Abukuma, Usugumo, Wakaba, Hatsushimo* and the *Hatsuharu* were about the same distance south of Attu. Each force stayed in their areas with exception of the flagship, *Abukuma,* which stood off the entrance to Holtz Bay.

The stevedores with their usual double-time marching with every item they could carry off the transports, had them unloaded and were on their way in about one hour. The cargo was air field construction materials and food and

Nojima Maru, bombed senseless during the war, still rests on the sand in Kiska harbor. (Lower) As viewed from the narrow beach in 1987.

Kiska harbor June 1942 shown in photograph from PBY. There are four ships including one burning.

was landed between the 10th and 15th of March. The fleet had its rendezvous for the run back to Paramushiro north of Attu to where it returned without damage. The captain of the *Usugumo* alerted the others that he thought he had picked up an American submarine near the entrance of Holtz Bay because of a sudden flash which he believed to have been a torpedo fired at him which exploded without hitting anything.

One of the other ships reported a radio message in plain language that Japanese ships were coming. The transmission was presumed to have been from the American submarine and it was about half an hour before the transports entered Holtz Bay.

The Battle of the Komondorskis

About the 24th of March the Fifth Fleet with the same organization and strength, but with an extra transport (*Sanko Maru*) sortied for a trip to Attu. Off Paramushiro it broke into in three groups. The *Sanko Maru*, escorted by the *Usugumo*, left a day early (23rd) due to its slow speed. Later that day were the *Asaka Maru* and the *Sakito Maru* and the ships of the 1st Destroyer Div. Not departing until the 24th was the main body consisting of heavy cruisers *Nachi*, *Maya* and light cruiser *Tama*, a 20-year old veteran. The second two groups rendezvoused in the afternoon of the 26th but little progress was made due to a raging sea. A radio message was sent out for regrouping a 1 a.m. on the 27th. The force was in column in this order. *Nachi*, *Maya*, *Tama*, *Wakaba*, *Hatsushimo*, *Abukuma*, *Ikazuchi*, *Inazuma*, *Asaka Maru* and *Sakito Maru*. The vessels maintained a separation of 600 meters except the destroyers were closer at 300 meters. The course was north.

One of the ships in the rear flashed a message that two silhouettes were seen, south, 6,000 to 8,000 meters. At 0313 it was determined what had been spotted were American ships bearing 160° true, distance 13½ miles. Because of the high bridge on *Nachi*, she probably saw the enemy at the same time. The *Nachi* immediately ordered the transports to separate from the convoy and retire to the west. The entire columns then changed to the east and then to the south with orders to assume battle formation.

The 1st Destroyer Div. formed with the *Abukuma* in the lead followed in column by *Wakaba*, *Hatsushimo*, *Ikazuchi*, then *Inazuma*. The wind was northeast at 7 knots. Battle action opened with a salvo from *Nachi*. The Americans opened fire very soon thereafter. *Nachi* fired torpedoes at the Americans who were to the southwest within three first 25 minutes of start of the engagement.

In the turn to the southwest then west, *Tama* cut inside the destroyers cut inside *Tama* with *Tama* coming out slightly in the lead on a westerly course by about 0430. The *Abukuma* was to the north between 0430 and 0500. *Abukuma* received most of the fire the American force. She fired her four port side torpedoes at a range of about 15, 000 meters then turned north. This placed *Abukuma* a little behind *Tama* and *Maya*. Between 0500 and 0600 the Americans laid a smoke screen so it was difficult for the Japanese to see the ships but occasionally glimpsed re seen.

About 0530 *Abukuma* received orders to cross astern and come up on the south side of *Nachi*. Because *Ikazuchi* and *Inazuma* were old (both completed in 1932) and slow, the group reduced speed to about 28 knots down from 30 knots. The smoke screen of the Americans was effective and the Japanese did not know if the American force would go to the north or south. If to the south, then the *Abukuma* and the destroyers with her would be closest. The Japanese continued to sail westward in an effort to fight the Americans. At 0615 *Abukuma* fired four starboard side torpedoes at a range of 16,000 meters. At about 0630 the force turned south and the *Abukuma* was again abreast of *Tama* and *Nachi* in formation.

The Japanese force continued westward with some zigzagging on the lookout for the American force and spotted them about 7 a.m. directly to the south of *Wakaba* and *Hatsushimo*. Each fired 6 torpedoes at a range about 16,000 meters. The Japanese believed these torpedoes went inside the group of ships but there was no observation of any hits. The torpedoes fired by *Nachi* and *Abukuma*, and the destroyers, were set for 32 knots which would give extreme range of 32,000 meters. These were Type 93, 24-inch diameter oxygen fish which left no wake.

At about 0615, a message, believed from Kiska, was received that ten-plus planes (bombers) were on their way. This was good news to the Japanese who wanted to hurry the battle because of low fuel capacity of the *Ikazuchi* and *Inazuma*.

The *Maya* and the *Nachi* had launched their observation planes early in the engagement but the pilots did not make effective reports due to the American-made smoke. Accordingly, the Japanese had no news of any damage they'd caused. About 7 a.m. they had a glimpse of a cruiser with a 15 degree list. The direction the cruiser, which was smoking, was heading could not be determined. The Japanese also spotted two destroyers smoking. A little later, the observation planes flashed messages that the cruiser with the list was dead in the water.

During this excitement there was a duel between *Nachi* and *Maya* and American destroyers. The Americans were seen to be firing very rapidly. Some torpedoes were fired at the Japanese but they did not know the source. These exploded prematurely at about 1,500 and 2,000 meters to the port side of *Abukuma*. If the torpedoes had not exploded too soon, the Japanese believe it would have been the end of their *Abukuma*.

A little after 7 o'clock, the Japanese broke off the engagement due to a report that American bombers were on the way. Another excuse for disengagement was the statement at the post-war interrogation: "because of low fuel capacity" of a number of the ships.

The *Abukuma*, with 6, 14cm guns, carried about 200 to 250 rounds per gun and she had plenty of ammunition left after the engagement. Each gun of *Tama* fired about 50 shells and there were about 150 rounds per gun remaining after disengagement. But the *Nachi* and the *Maya* had shot up nearly everything that had. By 0730 the Japanese were on a westerly course and the Americans were headed south.

Colonel Yamazaki's force was in the *Asaka Maru* and the *Sanko Maru* had mostly cargo and a few soldiers. In command at Attu at that time was Lt. Col. Yonekawa, to have been relieved with Col. Yamazaki's arrival. There were no troops embarked on any of the fighting ships. (Later, Col. Yamazaki reached Attu but on what ship and on what date was not recalled.)

The Japanese believed they damaged the cruiser and at least two or three destroyers but said they did not believe they sank anything. On their way from the scene of the battle, they came upon a large oil slick and at that time realized they had inflicted some serious damage on the American battle fleet.

The Japanese said they did not make any further destroyer escorted runs into Attu after the Battle of the Komondorskis but that submarines were supplying both Attu and Kiska. One or two destroyers did get into Attu early in April at the time Colonel Yamazaki was landed.

After the force returned to Paramushiro, flag was transferred to *Kiso* and *Abukuma* sailed for Maizuru for overhaul and arrived there about April 10. The cruiser got RADAR at this time.

The *Kiso* left Maizuru for Paramushiro with a stop at Ominato. She pulled in to Paramushiro about 20th of April. On May 9th, she left with *Wakaba* and *Hatsushimo* along with *Kimikawa Maru*, which was transporting seaplanes, for Kiska. The plan was for the convoy to proceed to a point about 250 miles southwest of Attu where the planes were to be launched then they would fly to Attu then on to Kiska. But the Japanese learned of the American invasion of Attu at about noon on 12 May so the plan was changed.

No planes were launched by the tender and the ship, with its planes still on board, was ordered back to Paramushiro by itself. The combat craft would proceed to Attu for an attack on the American landing force. But the run in to Attu would have to avoid daylight hours due to high risk of being seen and attacked by the Americans. The plan was issued to attack on the night of the 13th. But the Japanese were at such distance even if they sailed at top speed they would not arrive in time. It was decided to rally the force about 250 miles southwest of Attu. However another change was in store for that night the force was ordered to return to Paramushiro.

By the end of May, the situation at Attu had become definitely critical for the Japanese there. The small occupation force was being overrun by well-equipped Americans. With their supplies running low, the *Abukuma* and 4 destroyers were dispatched on 25th of May. The plan was to haul in the cargo then remove "important personages" These persons were the naval Communications Staff officer (a Commander Emoto), and one Army Staff Officer (name not known) who had gone to Attu from Hokkaido as an observer. The plot was to work past the American ships on the night of 29 May.

The force proceeded up to about 150 miles southwest of Attu but because the weather was clear, and there were no intelligence reports, the Japanese were afraid of being seen by American planes so delayed the dash into harbor for one day – the night of the 29th [*sic.*].

On Attu, Colonel Yamazaki radioed a message that his situation was "very grave" and the issue was in doubt. Accordingly, the Commander of the Fifth Fleet ordered the force to return to Paramushiro.

> Believing there was nothing the Japanese naval flotilla could do to relieve the losing situation on Attu, the garrison there was abandoned to face the American liberation forces the best it could.

The last Japanese surface ship to arrive in Kiska was a destroyer about the end of February or early March. After that, there was only submarine transport available. But two *I*-class subs were sunk south of Kiska. Hauling cargo by submarine was a very difficult proposition therefore in early June it was decided to withdraw the Japanese troops from that island by ship. Some evacuation of the Kiska force had already been been done by *I*-class submarine but this tied up submarines that were badly needed elsewhere and was too risky. One had been sunk with a full load of soldiers thus the matter of evacuation by surface craft was the only answer.

> Captain Arichika was directed to determine a method for evacuating the Japanese on Kiska then to do it. Every step of the evacuation had to be precise as the lives of over 5,000 men were at stake. Time was short.

Kiska Evacuated

Orders came from Vice Admiral Shiro Kawase, who was Commander of the Fifth Fleet, passed down from rear Admiral Masatyomi Kimura, then Commander 1st Destroyer Squadron, for Captain Arichika to formulate plans

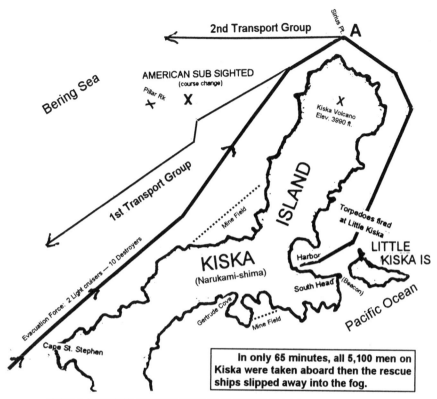

In only 65 minutes, all 5,100 men on Kiska were taken aboard then the rescue ships slipped away into the fog.

KISKA ACCESS ROUTE FOR EVACUATION OF JAPANESE TROOPS
Arrival and departure on same track from point A into harbor

for the evacuation. The troops were to be away from Kiska by July. He was assigned a fleet made up of cruisers *Abukuma, Kiso, Tama,* the 6th destroyer Div (*Ikazuchi, Inazuma*), the 21st Destroyer Div. (*Wakaba, Hatsushimo*), the 9th Destroyer Div. (*Asagumo, Usugumo, Hibiki*) as well as converted cruisers *Asaka Maru* and *Awata Maru.* But the last two ships were too slow for an operation of dash in, dash out as this would be, and cruiser *Tama* was declared to be "too old and unreliable."

Captain Arichika felt he needed more destroyers so requested them He was given 6 more. The High Command felt the evacuation was important and also urgent (there were over 5,000 men on Kiska). Tokyo gave him the 10th Destroyer Division in excxhange for the 6th Destroyer Division. This new division was made up of: *Yugumo, Kazagumo, Akigumo* plus independent group *Shimakaze, Naganami* and *Samidare.* The 6th Destroyer Division (only 2 ships) was ordered back to Japan. In the swap, Captain Arichika gained 4 destroyers.

On 7 July the cruisers *Abukuma* and *Kiso* left Paramushiro with the 9th, 10th and 21st Destroyers Divisions and the three independants. Also along

201

was a tanker (*Nihon Maru*) which had its own escort, a coast defense picket boat the *Kunajiri*.

This fleet went to position about 200 miles southwest of Kiska where it was on station until early July waiting for its change to sneak in, but it returned to Paramushiro due to unfavorable weather – clear.No good for evacuating troops without being seen. What was desired was a very foggy day.

The flotilla left Paramushiro on the 22 at 2010 hours and ran to rendezvous at 46° 30' N then east to 170° and waited in that area for the summer fog to thicken.

> At 1700 on 26th of July, *Kunajiri* and *Abukuma* had a severe "fender-bender" in the fog. In the midst of this confusion *Wakaba* and *Naganami* also collided! The damage was such that the *Kunajiri* and the *Wakaba* were ordered to the body shop, without escort, at best capabilities – 9 knots – all the way back to Japan.

The force's position at 0000 on 28th of July was roughly at 46° 40' N - 173° 10' E. From that point the vessels made a direct run on course 20° True to a point 15 miles from Cape Stephen. Here, the slower *Tama* was sent back to Paramushiro. The rest of the ships, actually glimpsing Cape St. Stephen at about 10 a.m. on the 29th for a few minutes, continued slowly on soundings as they went due to unsure depth of the water about one mile off shore. The ships stayed on this route until they reached the indentation on the west side of Kiska. Then they headed for a point one mile off shore near Kiska volcano. The force then circumnavigated the north end of Kiska, still about one mile off shore, then made a dash in the fog directly into Kiska Harbor. It had been agreed with the land force earlier to set up a beacon on Kiska's South Head.

The trip inbound was uneventful from an enemy learning that they were there standpoint. There was risk of collision in the fog and lack of knowledge about the water on this uncommon approach to the harbor.

But there was excitement when *Abukuma* thought there was an American cruiser in the way and promptly fired 4 torpedoes at what turned out to be Little Kiska Island. Two of the fish exploded when they hit the island and two traveled on to hit South Head.

A a detractor for identification from a distance, the center smoke stack on the *Abukuma* had been painted white so in fog it would appear to be a two-stacked vessel.

At 1340, all but pickets went in and anchored at the inshore end of the harbor. *Hibiki* took guard station off Little Kiska. *Shimakaze, Naganami* and *Samidare* maintained a steady patrol off the entrance to the harbor. The visibility inside the harbor was good.

Each destroyer carried one handing boat and the cruisers each had two. There were several landing craft at Kiska and all were used to move the evacuees quickly. When everyone was on board, the small boats were sunk. Of the personnel to be evacuated, 450 went onto each destroyer and 1,200 on each cruiser. The flotilla steamed away at 1435 hours in two groups. The first was of *Abukuma, Yugumo, Kazagumo, Akigumo, Shimakaze, Samidare*. The

(Clockwise) Vice Admiral S. Kawase, Commander 5th Fleet. He went with Kiska evacuation fleet as observer. Rear Admiral Masatomi Kimura, Commander Kiska evacuation project and Commander 1st Destroyer Squadron. The evacuation was "a bold, risky move carried out with precision." Rear Admiral Boshiro Hosogaya, Commander Northern Area Task Force. The Battle of the Komondorskis was his undoing.

second group was *Kiso, Asagumo, Usugumo, Hibiki, Hatsushimo, Abukuma*. The track out was the same as the track inbound north of Kiska volcano. The *Abukuma* group proceeded midway between Kiska and Pillar Rock then southwest.

At a point two miles south but east of Pillar Rock, an American submarine surfaced at about 2,000 meters from *Abukuma*. In a quick movement, the cruiser led the group in a 45 degree angle turn away. The American submarine submerged apparently never having seen the fleet in the fog. The course resumed and the *Abukuma* group moved along at 28 knots on approximate course 210° True to 48th parallel thence along that line to about 159° E then went directly for Paramushiro. The ships pulled in on August 1st.

The group led by *Kiso* went south only as far as 50° N then followed directly into Paramushiro arriving on July 31.

The senior duty officer among those evacuated from Kiska was Rear Admiral Katsuzo Akiyama. The Senior Army officer was Major General Mineki. The Japanese left only three dogs on Kiska. The last men to leave the island set up timed explosives to detonate a few days later to give the impression that troops were still there and going about daily business.

気のため　後輩に　ゆづりました。

The Kiska Memorial Association

The members are those veterans of the Imperial Navy and Army who were stationed on Kiska and on Attu. The association holds regular reunions. Seichi Kakizaki, a veteran of the Kiska occupation, was president of the Kiska Memorial Association for three years. He wrote to the author saying the Association has made a great effort to collect diaries of individual soldiers for the sake of history from which a small booklet was published. In 1980 those members who were able returned to Kiska (Narukami Shima) for sentimental reunion where life during the Pacific War was very difficult.

Seichi Kakizaki closed his letter with two short statements:

1. The No. 1 failure of the Japanese Aleutian Operation was we could not build air strip as all heavy equipment had been sent into the South Seas

2. About the daring evacuation of Kiska, "Thank God for the Men who got out."

Appendix A
Admiral James Sargent Russell, U. S. N.
(Retired)

Jim Russell was born in Tacoma, Washington on the 22nd of March 1903 to Ambrose J. and Loella Janet (Sargent) Russell. On April 13, 1929 he married Dorothy Irene Johnson who died 18 April 1965. Their children: Donald Johnson and Kenneth McDonald. He married a widow, Geraldine Haus Rahn on July 12, 1966. She had two children, Fred and Barbara.

As a youngster, Russell attended DeKoven Hall Boys School and Stadium High School, Tacoma from which he graduated at age 15. He attempted to enlist in the Navy in 1918 but he was declared to be too young, however he joined the Merchant Marine and he saw sea duty in the First World War.

In 1922 he received an appointment to the U. S. Naval Academy from Congressman Albert Johnson, 3rd District, Washington State. Russell was a serious scholar at the Academy and graduated in 1926, 15th in his class of 456. His first duty was on the battleship *West Virginia* for two years, a requirement before he would be allowed to attend flying school. He received his wings as a Naval Pilot on July 10th, 1929 as Naval Aviator No. 3495.

Russell qualified in aircraft carrier landings aboard the U.S.S. *Langley* (CV-1), the first American aircraft carrier, in a Vought F-1 biplane in November 1929. This fabric covered airplane had a 220-hp Wright J-3 engine and could fly up to 153 mph. He later flew in various aircraft including float planes, flying boats, fighter-bombers and performed aviation shipboard duty. His flying experiences included piloting the Vought scouts, (Kingfishers on wheels and floats); Keystone; Douglas and Consolidated flying boats; Sikorski, Loening and Grumman amphibians; Curtis, Boeing, Vought and Grumman fighters plus various turbo-props and jets.

The Navy sent him to California Technical Institute in Pasadena, California where he graduated with a Master of Science Degree in Aero-Engineering in 1935. Just before and during the early part of World War II, Russell commanded Naval Patrol Squadron 42 in Alaska with duty that extended all the way to Attu.

In December 1942 he was reassigned to the Navy Department in Washington. D. C., to head a study for advanced air bases as were envisioned for "island-hopping" in the Pacific. Next he was Director of Military Requirements for the Bureau of Aeronautics. In June 1944 he returned to sea duty as Chief of Staff of Rear Admiral Ralph Davison, Commander Carrier Division 2 and one of Admiral Marc A. Mitchener's Fast Carrier Task Force Group Commanders. As Chief of Staff to Admiral R. E. Davison, Russell engaged in the Campaigns of the Palau Islands, the Philippines, Iwo Jima and Okinawa.

After the surrender of Japan, he went immediately into Japan first on Technical Air Intelligence then with the Naval Analysis Division of the U.S. Strategic Bombing Survey. In these two assignments he was privileged to interview former enemy personnel on their roles in the Pacific War.

Russell was later Commander of U.S.S. *Bairoko* (CVE-115) and then U.S.S. *Coral Sea* (CVE-43). He had 3½ years on the staff of the U.S. Atomic Energy Commission in charge for the Commission of its task Group at Eniwetok in the first weapons development tests there (Operation Sandstone).

He later commanded Anti-Submarine Warfare Carrier Division 17, then Attack Carrier Division 5 in the Western Pacific. He was Chief of the Navy Bureau of Aeronautics 1955-1957. While in that office, he was awarded the

Collier Trophy for 1956 sharing the award with Mr. C. J. McCarthy of Chance Vought Co., the outstanding contribution to aviation in that year for development of the supersonic Crusader Navy fighter plane, the first ship-based aircraft to fly faster than 1,000 miles per hour.

In 1957-58 Russell, as Vice Admiral, was Deputy Commander, Atlantic Fleet. Then he served as Vice Chief of Naval Operations as Admiral (4 stars) 1958-1961 under Admiral Arleigh Burke, Chief of Naval Operations. From 1962-65 he was Commander-in-Chief of NATO Forces in Southern Europe charged with the defense of the NATO southern flank in Italy, Greece and Turkey. Admiral Russell retired on April 1, 1965 following 43 years of active service.

During the years 1965-79 he served as a part-time consultant to Boeing Aircraft Company. In August 1967, the Navy recalled him to active duty to review safety in aircraft carrier operations in the Gulf of Tonkin. He was again recalled to duty, when in 1968, as chairman of a study group for the Secretary of Defense, he made a second visit to the SE Asia Theater.

Decorations: Distinguished Service Medal with Oak Leaf Cluster; Legion of Merit with 2 Oak Leaf Clusters; Distinguished Flying Cross; Air Medal (U.S.); Grand Cross Royal Order King George I (Greece); Grand Official Order Republic of Italy; Commander, Legion of Honor (France); Great Cross Peruvian Cross of Naval Merit; Grand Officer Order of Naval Merit (Brazil); recipient Collier Trophy, 1956; Russell Trophy Order of Daedalians; Named to National Museum of Naval Aviation Hall of Honor 1990; Fellow American Institute of Aero and Astronautics. His service medals include Asiatic-Pacific Medal with 4 battle stars, American Defense Medal with service star, American Theater Medal, WWII Victory Medal.

Admiral Russell lives in retirement with his wife in a serene setting on the shore of American Lake near Tacoma, Washington. He and Dorothy produced two sons, five grandchildren, three grand-grandchildren. His second wide, Geraldine, had a son and a daughter who had six children. ❖

Appendix B
The "Battle of the Pips"

> The Kiska Evacuation was successful because of Japanese savvy, American bungling, Aleutian weather and good fortune.
> —Morison Vol. VII. p. 59

A patrolling PBY on a search 200 miles southwest of Attu radioed on July 23rd of a contact made on seven ships. Two destroyers, the *Aylwin* and the *Monaghan*, that were on Kiska harbor blockade, were summoned to join a force of other warships including battleships *Mississippi* and *Idaho* and cruisers *Portland* and *Wichita*, every one of these ships also having picked up the RADAR pips. With the two destroyers pulled off Kiska harbor patrol, this left the door open. When the pips were just 8 miles from the advance cruisers and 12 miles from the battle wagons Rear Admiral R. C. "Ike" Giffin, the force commander, ordered firing to start. It was 7 minutes after midnight on July 26.

These capitol ships opened fire with 14-inch and 8-inch guns based on the RADAR contact. If there was something odd about all this it was that cruiser *San Francisco* and all of the destroyers, never did have pips show on their RADAR scopes. The RADAR screens that had been following the battle all reported loss of contacts at 12:44 a.m. so the firing stopped It seemed like a quick victory. The battleships had salvoed 518 rounds of 14-inch shells and the cruisers expended 487 of their 8-inch shells.

A Kingfisher spotter plane was catapulted at dawn to survey the damage. The pilot when to the scene, based on the pips and reported only clear, tossing seas. No wreckage. No oil slicks. Nothing! The whole affair was dubbed "The Battle of the Pips." While this American battle force was collecting itself and refueling from tanker *Pecos* 105 miles southeast of Kiska, Admiral Kimura made his run to the north of Kiska, circled the island, entered the bay, snatched up all living souls and disappeared into the fog just 65 minutes after dropping anchor.

Appendix C
Two Who Died
One From Each Side

"Cap" Collier

Paul N. Tatsuguchi, M.D., graduated from Pacific Union College, Angwin, California, then he earned his doctorate at Loma Linda University in 1938. Later, while serving as a Christian medical missionary in Japan where he lived with his wife and daughter, he was conscripted into the Japanese Army against his will. He did not believe in war. Although he was a physician and surgeon licensed in California (No. 8161), the Japanese authorities didn't like him for his "American ways" so he was not allowed to be an officer. He was assigned as a surgeon in the field hospital on Attu.

When it was obvious that Japan had lost its control of Attu and that the invading Americans would win the issue, he wrote in his diary, "Banzai to Emperor...good-bye Taeko, by beloved wife...only 33 years of living and I am to die here."

In the final battle of Attu when U. S. troops captured his hospital, Dr. Tatsuguchi, trying to shout louder than the noises of battle, in clear English and waving his Bible, was shot and killed.

On April 16, 1988, Mrs. Tatsuguchi was presented with a posthumous "Honored Alumnus" award for her late husband from Pacific Union College.

There is in Japan today, a "Kiska Memorial Association" whose members meet annually. At a recent reunion there were over 200 present. Survivors from Attu number a mere handful—those transferred before the liberation and a few who were prisoners.

Allen C. Collier, Jr., Arkansas, was the bugler for Headquarters Company, 206th Coast Artillery (AA). He was standing at the flag pole ready to sound a call when he was killed by fragments from a bomb during the Japanese attack on Dutch Harbor on June 3, 1942. He is buried in Sitka National Cemetery. Collier's First Sergeant retrieved the damaged bugle and sent it to Collier's parents as a memorial, but the bugle was lost a few years ago in a fire.

(See page 40.)

Appendix D
Adak National Forest

Most items hauled into the Aleutian chain of islands during World War II have disappeared for various reasons except for some then seedling trees. General Buckner was interested in co-operating with the U. S. Forest Service to see if trees would grow in these volcanic islands. In June 1944, a Captain W. E. Maurin took Dr. David Bruce of the Forest Service on a tour of Adak looking at the few living trees there.

In 1945, 4,000 spruce seedlings were supposed to be shipped to six islands as part of a planting program. The only trees presently identified from this project have been slowly growing in a patch about a quarter of an acre in size on Adak. Apparently Captain Bruce either planted or supervised the planting then he protected them with burlap on stakes forming a "box" around each seedling. This was for protection from wind and drifting snow. In 1964, the trees were between 4 and 12 feet tall. By 1990 some of the trees had reached 16 feet.

The Adak "National Forest" is an informal name given to this patch but the Forest Service does not show it on any list and most of its workers say they never heard of it (and some even seem to sneer when told the Adak National Forest exists).

At Adak is indeed the only "National Forest" that has every tree in it lighted at Christmas, a project of the Adak Kiwanis Club.

"A touch of home," said a female Navy oceanographer from western Oregon who was stationed at Adak. "If it wasn't for those trees, I think I'd go nuts here." (Lower) The Adak Kiwanis Club strings over 2,000 twinkling lights on the "forest" each Christmas.

Appendix E
Memorial at Dutch Harbor

**WORLD WAR II
IN THE ALEUTIANS**
THIS MONUMENT IS DEDICATED TO
THOSE WHO SUFFERED
AND KNEW THE PAIN OF WAR
TO THOSE WHO DIED
TO THE MANY WHO DEFENDED
THEIR COUNTRY BRAVELY.
THIS MONUMENT
IS IN YOUR HONOR.
ALEUT CIVILIANS
U.S. MILITARY PERSONNEL
CANADIAN MILITARY PERSONNEL
JAPANESE MILITARY PERSONNEL
1942 — 1945

Memorial dedicated in June 1982 by Admiral Russell, USN (ret) (center); Colonel Abe and Admiral Samejima (left and right) at Dutch Harbor. Colonel Abe was still upset that American P-40 fighter planes from secret Umnak airstrip just 40 miles from Dutch harbor attacked his planes so, a special flight was arranged to take him to see the remains of the Umnak strip. (See page 47.)

Notes

The experience in the Aleutians proved to be a training ground for men from Generals to buck Privates, from Admirals to seamen as many of them had later battle tours in the South Pacific (a chance to get warm after freezing in Alaska) and a large number found themselves in Europe. Some did not survive the war.

General Simon Bolivar Buckner, Jr., finished his assignment in Alaska with the ousting of the Japanese then later led the 10th Army's invasion of Okinawa. Always a man to want to be in the thick of the action, he was visiting his troops when he was killed while in a forward position on Okinawa.

General Charles H. Corlett went from the Kiska invasion to another invasion to conquer Kwajalein and other islands in the Marshals. This time the Japanese were waiting. Later in England, he took part in the planning for the invasion of fortress Europe.

Captain Leslie H. Gehres became skipper of the carrier *Franklin*. He had a very hot time when the ship was bombed by Japanese aircraft in the Ryukyu Islands.

Lt. Cdr. James S. Russell, to whom this book is dedicated, went to Washington D.C. and also to Japan. He served a full career in the Navy and enjoys retirement near Tacoma. His biographical sketch is Appendix A.

After Admiral Robert A. Theobald left Alaskan duty, he became commander of the 1st Naval District with office in the Boston Navy Yard.

Lt. Cdr. Hiroishi Samejima, who led the Japanese attack on Dutch Harbor, stayed in the Navy, saw it transformed to become the post-war Japanese Maritime Self-Defense Force of which he rose to become its commander when I visited with him in Tokyo in 1975.

General John L. DeWitt, an able administrator, was needed at his desk thus he did not participate in the "shooting" war – with one almost chance to at least witness some action. For the Kiska invasion, he left Adak on a destroyer then transferred to a small boat to witness the landing from the battleship *Pennsylvania*. Since the Japanese had slipped away from Kiska in the fog, DeWitt was robbed of his chance to see a fight.

> The authors have been unable to determine the name of the destroyer on which General DeWitt sailed between Adak and Kiska. Readers who have such information are urged to write to the publisher. The address is on page iv.

The quote from Gen. Billy Mitchell is in Garfield (1982) p.49; Potter pp. 12-13, 74.

Japanese fishing in Alaskan waters is in Potter pp. 14-17; Clark, Henry W., *Alaska the Last Frontier*. Grossett (1930) pp. 172, 173-174, 206-photo.

Shortage of information about Aleutian tides, locations, etc., in Japanese hands at the start of the war are in letters from Hasagawa to the authors and personal interview in Tokyo. He was one of the *I*-boat captains ordered to search for data in his *I-26*.

Bert Webber and Admiral Hiroichi Samejima discuss details about the *Aleutian Headache* in the Admiral's office in Tokyo.

For the description of Adm. Theobald, see Garfield pp. 13ff. We did not find any biographical records on the admiral when we visited the Boston Navy Yard in 1989, but his name, along with other commanders who served there, is on a bronze tablet in the front yard of the headquarters building.

Data about the use of PBY Catalina aircraft is in many sources including Garfield; Cohen; Morison and in collaboration with Admiral Russell from 1972 to the present time.

Description of Fort Greely and Fujita's flight over Kodiak NAS is in several Webber books but the most recent is *Siege -III* (1992) and from Fujita personal interviews in 1975, 1987, 1990.

About the Army telephone switchboard shown on page 15. This is the second of three boards. The first was the suitcase model. It was a non-electric field switchboard of limited capacity (40 lines) never intended for long-time use. The photo is of a single position (1 operator) Western Electric standard switch-board (100 lines) which also soon outgrew its usefulness. A small building intended specifically for a telephone exchange was snuggled against the side of a hill into which this switchboard was moved along with three additional positions. It was common to use two operators as each position overlapped. The Chief Operator, of the 4-position board, was Sergeant George Cole (not shown) who, at a nearby desk, handled complaints. The men in the picture (made by the author), are Tim Desmond, civilian installer; Sgt. Charles S. "Windy" Schaeffer, Wire Chief; Pvt Jerry Hewitt, operator; Cpl. Dale L. Ramm, Chief Operator; Sgt. Richard H. Gardner, outside construction chief; Cpl. Eugene Tolliver, operator at the board. After the war, the entire telephone system was sold and moved into Kodiak where it was used until it was converted to dial. During the war there were only three lines from the

214

Army to town. These went to Kraft's General Store and dock, to the Alaska Communications System office and to the Bank of Kodiak.

The devotion to duty and anecdotes about Col. W. O. Eareckson are in Garfield and from my several talks with Admiral Russell. Eareckson, the one-man blitz with bomber command, could fly any airplane. He was transferred to Pearl Harbor then to New Guinea. At Pearl, Admiral Nimitz honored this Air Force officer with the Navy Cross. By the end of the war, Eareckson had been awarded every medal except the Congressional Medal of Honor. It does not seem generally known that while at Adak, Eareckson wrote poetry at least some of which was set to music! (See page 141.)

Admiral Samejima provided translations about deployment of *I*-class submarines to us though Admiral Russell as early as 1972. Admiral Samejima and I collaborated further in Tokyo in 1975. His bombing near the radio shack at Dutch Harbor will be found in Stanton H. Patty's piece in *Seattle Times,* "Former Japanese Raider to Attend Reunion of Aleutian Patrol Wing." Aug. 13, 1972. p. E-2.

Salvage of the captured, damaged Zero fighter plane is in various sources but a fine detailed account of in-air, side-by-side (dog fights) testing of it and many U.S. fighters in Southern California is in Ethell, pp. 601-606. U.S. planes pitted against the Zero (Mitsubishi A6M2) were P38F; P-39D-1; P-5l; P-40F; F4F-4; F4U-1. The quotation from Jiro Horikoshi is from his book *Eagles of Mitsubishi.*

Capture and interrogation of Lt. Hunt by Japanese is in Garfield, pp. 32, 39; and was vividly recalled during talks with Admiral Russell in Sept. 1983 as were his recollections of the "Kiska Blitz." This event also appear in Garfield, pp. 85-89.

Details of the intrigue of code breaking is in many places. We depended primarily on Lewis, Kahn and Zacharias.

American submarines on patrol in Alaska waters are in numerous sources. We consulted Holmes as well Morison.

Stories about Japanese submarines are in many sources with various degrees of validity. We believe the most dependable to be (in any order) Watts and Gordon, Morison, Holmes.

Admiral Theobald's fleet of fourteen ships in which he set out to bombard Kiska, then didn't fire, is in Morison VIII p.9. His quote "sick of the navy," etc., is in Garfield p. 127.

Evacuation of Guadalcanal by the Japanese is in Merillat, Herbert H., *Guadalcanal Remembered.* Dodd (1982). pp. 234-236. Admiral Nimitz quoted on p. 236.

Rear Admiral Thomas C. Kinkaid biosketch is in Morison V, p.88; his Aleutian duty described in many sources including Garfield; Morison.

Capture of Attu is in Morison VII, p.19-21; Garfield, pp. 199-214; Cohen, pp. 188-205; also in Love, Edmond G., *A History of the 7th Infantry* "Part II: Attu," Inf. Jour. Press. 1950. pp. 9-98. Interview with B. T. "Ted" Schwartz, Central Point, Ore., who landed on Attu on D+2, Sept. 1983.

Of Bill Macbeth's anecdotes of his war duty, one had to do with his arrival at Fort Richardson and his introduction to what another officer apparently thought of service there. When Bill got to the barracks about 10:30 at night, in bright daylight, the driver unloaded the luggage from the car and placed it on the ground under a small second floor balcony. There suddenly appeared on the balcony a fellow, "completely nude and completely out of his gourd from drinking – urinated over the edge of the balcony. We yelled, cursed to no avail. When he completed violating our luggage he disappeared Later I figured out he was demonstrating 'Welcome to the Alaska Theater!'" Macbeth was to "Go West Young Man" all the way to Shemya and Attu. At Shemya we was Provost Marshall and Base Utilities Officer. On Attu he was, among other jobs, Acting Commanding Officer at Alexai Point Air Base.

The intriguing material about Dr. Paul Tatsuguchi, MD is from a Seventh-Day Adventist publication, *Scope,* July-Sept. 1981 pp. 20-22; reinforced by Archives at Pacific Union College, Anguin, Calif. and from Loma Linda Univ., Calif. The Dept. of Consumer Affairs State of Calif., Sacramento, determined that Dr. Tatsugushi held a valid medical license in California in 1938.

Battle of Komondorski Islands is in Lorelli; Morison VII pp 22-36; Garfield pp. 178ff; Holmes p. 216 and in USSBS No. 367 *Aleutian Campaign....* upon which we depended for the Japanese side of the subject (Chapter 22).

The hassle of selecting an Army commander for Attu liberation is in Garfield p.204.

Alaska Scout's arrival on Attu in submarines *Narwhal* and *Nautilus* is in Garfield p. 208, 212-213, 215; and other sources. Some writers indicate the Alaska Scouts were part of the 7th Inf, which is erroneous.

The raming and sinking of *I-24* off Shemya by Lt. Wm. G. Cornell is in Watts & Gordon pp. 334 as occurring May 12, 1943. Garfield p. 281 and Hashimoto's, book *Sunk!* errs by placing *I-24* in Admiralty Islands and in July.

軍が決める救出作戦を行ひ…
共同
ロサンゼルス十三日
旧日本軍の潜水艦発見
太平洋戦争で旧日本…

The *Yomiuri Shimbun* on Oct 13, 1989 had a story out of Los Angeles saying the U.S. Navy and National Park Service discovered "six (6) *RO-65*-type submarines 800 meters off [Kiska] in 30 meters depth. The bow of the subs are damaged by U. S. Navy air raid."

What really happened was a single sub, the *RO-65*, was attacked by U.S. bombs. *RO-65* submerged but was never hit. While undersea, *RO-65* hit a rock then sank on Apr. 11, 1942.

Detailed data regarding operations including losses in Aleutians is in the Japanese language work *Sehsuio socho [The Aleutians].* Appended in packet are charts of which major naval actions are tracked. Admiral Samejima translated portions of this major work for our use for which we thank him.

Evacuation of Japanese troops from Kiska (they named the island Narukami-shima) is in many sources including Garfield, pp. 280-283; Cohen, pp. 208, 210-211; Morison VII, pp. 56-64. Our data is directly from USSBS No. 367. Admiral Russell, at the time a Captain, was the interrogator. ❖

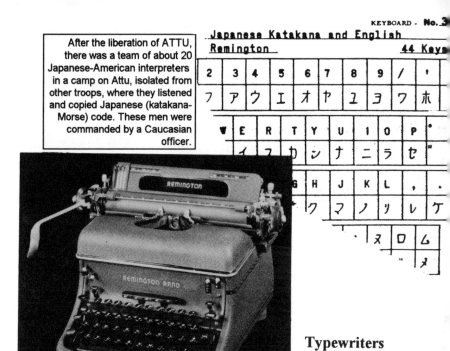

After the liberation of ATTU, there was a team of about 20 Japanese-American interpreters in a camp on Attu, isolated from other troops, where they listened and copied Japanese (katakana-Morse) code. These men were commanded by a Caucasian officer.

Japanese Katakana and English
Remington — **44 Keys**

Typewriters in the Aleutians

There were five brands of typewriters in military use with issue based on availability not brand preference. Many came with the units from the states. The most heavy duty and dependable was the Remington Rand "Model Seventeen" (shown). Most had "pica" type (10 letters to one inch) as this size type smashed through up to 10 carbon copies at one time. Royal KMM secretarial models had lighter touch but most Orderly Rooms did not have touch typists thus speed was not important. Underwood was a heavy typewriter, an older design, and L. C. Smith, older, were not often seen in the Aleutians. The Woodstock weighed a lot, was sluggish to use and was often relegated to non-essential desks. The Ordinance Department was responsible for repairs but these machines seldom needed fixing and were easy to work on. The Navy had a few early IBM Electromatic typewriters. These required trained typists. When a machine quit, it was hustled onto a Seattle-bound airplane for repair.

Remington and Underwood offered combination keyboards with English on the "shift" position and Katakana on the lower position. Katakana/English typewriters could be used for either language. These typewriters were popular with radio operators who "copied" Katakana-Morse code in either Japanese or English.

Bert Webber

About the Author

Bert Webber is a Research Photojournalist who has been writing and making photographs since he was a teenager. He served in the Regular U. S. Army from September 10, 1940 until honorably discharged on November 25, 1945. In addition to serving in the American Theater (U.S. mainland), he was in Alaska, Scotland, England, Belgium and France.

At the time he went to Alaska, six months before the start of WW-II, he and others of the small Signal Corps detachment at Kodiak fairley well handled whatever tasks came up but when Fort Greely's population exploded, each man went to a specialty. Webber handled switchboard work and was the Signal Corps photographer.

After 22 months at Fort Greely, he was accepted into aircrew training as pilot and did his preflight studies at the University of Nevada and at Santa Ana Army Air Base. He moved to Rankin Aeronautical Academy (Stearman PT-17) at Tulare where stunt pilot Tex Rankin was one of his primary instructors. Then he went to Minter Field at Bakersfield in BT-13 (Vultee Vibrators) and UC-78 twin engine. He was to train in B-25's at LaHunta when he was requested by the Signal Corps to attend the senior cameraman school at Paramount Studies, Astoria, New York. He trained there as a 35mm and 16mm newsreel cameraman. Webber went to Europe to shoot pictures for the Signal Corps in Southhampton, Verviers, Paris and Marsailles.

After the war he conducted a commercial photographic business and owned a camera shop for ten years in Sedro-Woolley, Washington. He later joined Remington Rand as a typewriter sales specialist staying for six years when he was offered admittance to Whitworth College, Spokane. There he refined his writing skills as a journalism major, studied librarianship and was certified to teach. He was Chief of Photo Services at the college and taught some photography classes.

Following graduation, he became a school librarian at Waluga Jr. High School in Lake Oswego, Oregon and earned the Master of Library Science Degree by attending night school at Portland State University and the University of Portland. He was the Head Librarian at Medford Senior High School but resigned to follow full-time research photojournalism in 1970.

Since that time he has written 40 books primarily about Oregon and the Oregon Trail including five books dealing with WW-II. His research into the Japanese attacks against the mainland of the United States has appeared in four separate books since 1975. The newest, *Silent Siege III, Japanese Attacks On North America in World War II*, was published in 1992.

Bert Webber is listed in *Who's Who in the West* and in *Contemporary Authors*. He and his wife, Margie, own Webb Research Group, publishers, and Pacific Northwest Books Co., distributors.

Bert and Margie Webber live in Oregon's Rogue River Valley. They have four children and at the moment seven grand children.

Illustration Credits

Cover, (top) author collection (ac); (lower) Adm. James S. Russell collection (JSRc)
ii, author
vi, (JSRc)
8, ac
9, (top) ac; (lower) A. Feitelberg coll. (AFc)
10, author
11, (top, lower right) author; (lower left) (AFc)
13, author
15, (left) author; (right) author from AFc
21, ac
26, (JSRc)
28, (top) author; (lower) Nichimo mini-craft models
29, ac
31, (JSRc)
32, ac
34, author
36-38, ac
39, (JSRc)
41, ac
42, V.O. Smith coll.
43, F.E.Fox, coll.
44, (top) Mike Mark; coll.; (lower) Leonard Lukens coll. (LLc)
46-47, (JSRc)
50, (JSRc)
54, (JSRc)
56, (JSRc); (lower) ac
59, ac
60-61, Clare Hanawalt collection (CHc)
62, ac
63, (top), ac; (lower), Don McArthor co (DMc)
64-65, (DMc)
66 (top) ac; (lower) (JSRc)
68, ac
70, ac
72, ac
74, ac
82, (JSRc)
86, ac
87, (CHc)
88, author
89, ac
93, (JSRc)
94, ac
95, author
96-98, ac
100, Wm. G. Macbeth coll. (WGMc)
102 103, ac
104, ac
105, ac
106, ac
107, (top) ac; (lower) Earl Reichert coll.
109, (top) ac; (center) (WGMc); (lower) ac
110, ac
111, (top) Mike Mark coll.; (lower) ac

112-113, (CHc)
114, (top) (WGMc); (lower) ac
115, Wayne B. Gentry coll. (WGBc)
116, (top) ac; (lower) (WGMc)
117, (top) (WGMc); (lower) ac
119, (WGMc)
120, (top and center) (WGMc); (lower) (WGMc)
121, (WBGc)
122, (top) ac; (lower) (WGMc)
123, (top) Cliff Johnson; (lower) (WGMc)
124, (top) Mike Mark; (lower) (WGMc)
125-126, (WGMc)
127, (top) (DMc); (lower) (WGMc)
128, (top) (DMc); (lower) (WGMc)
129, (top and center) Paul E. Malo; (lower)
130-131, (WGMc)
132, author
134, ac
138, (top) (CHc); (lower) ac
141, (CHc)
142, (AFc)
143, (top and center) (DMc); (lower) (CHc)
144; (DMc)
145, (top) (CHc); (center) (CHc); (lower) (DMc)
146, (top) (ac); (center) (DMc); (lower) ac
147, (top) (CHc); (lower) Evan V. Klett
149, (DMc)
150, (top and center) (DMc); (lower) ac
151, (top) (WBGc); (center and lower) (DMc);
152-154, (CHc)
155, (top) (WGMc); (lower) (WGMc)
156 -157, (CHc)
158-159, (DMc)
160, (top) (WBGc); (lower) (LLc)
163-172 (LLc)
175, James W. Spencer (JWSc)
176, (DMc)
177, (JWSc)
180, (top) (JSRc); (lower) (JWSc)
181, (JSRc)
182-183, U.S.Navy History Center
184, (top) ac; (lower) Col. Zenji Abe
186-187, 189, U.S. Navy History Center
195 (WGMc)
196, (top) ac; (lower) (DMc)
197, (CHc)
201, author
203, ac
205, (JSRc)
209, ((left) ac; (right) Oscar Jones
210, ac
211, Evan V. Klett
212, (JSRc)
214, Margie Webber
218, ac

Bibliography

Baker, Lillian. *American and Japanese Relocation in World War II Fact, Fiction & Fallacy.* Webb Research Group. 1990.

Bridgman, Leonard. *Janes All The World's Aircraft 1943-44.* Macmillan. 1945

Cohen, Stan[ley]. *The Forgotten War* [Alaska]. Pictorial Histories Co. 1981.

Conn, Stetson, Rose C. Engleman and Byron Fairchild. *Guarding the United States and Its Outposts, U. S. Army in World War II; The Western Hemisphere.* Chief of Mil. Hist., Dept. of the Army. 1964.

Craven, Wesley and Frank and James Lea Cate. *The Army Air Forces in World War II.* Vol. I. Univ of Chicago Press. 1948.

Dod, Karl. *The Corps of Engineers; The War Against Japan; The U.S. Army in World War II.* Chief of Mil. Hist., Dept. of the Army. 1966.

Dufresne, Frank. *My Way Was North; An Alaskan Autobiography.* Holt, Rinehart and Winston. 1966.

Ethel, Jeffrey L. (*et al.*) *The Great Book of World War II Airplanes.* Bonanza. 1984.

Garfield, Brian. *The Thousand Mill War; World War II in Alaska and the Aleutians.* Bantam. 1982.

Gruening, Ernest. *The State of Alaska.* Random House. 1954.

Holmes, W. J[asper]. *Undersea Victory; The Influence of Submarine Operations on the War in the Pacific.* Doubleday. 1966,

Horikoshi, Jiro. *Eagles of Mitsubishi.* U. of Wash. Press. 1981. p. 136.

Kahn, David. *The Code Breakers.* Signet. 1967.

Lewin, Ronald. *The American Magic; Codes, Ciphers and Defeat of Japan.* Farrar. 1982.

Leyton, Edwin T., *"And I Was There."* Quill/Morrow. 1986.

Lorelli, John A. *The Battle of the Komondorski Islands.* Naval Inst. Press. 1984.

McCombs, Don and Fred L. Worth. *World War II Super Facts.* Warner. 1983.

Morgan, Lael. *The Aleutians.* [Series No. 7] Alaska Geographic. 1980

Morison, Samuel Eliot. *History of United States Naval Operations in World War II.* Vol. 4. 1959; Vol. 7. 1964; Vol. 15. Atlantic Little Brown. 1962.

Roscoe, Theodore. *United States Destroyer Operations in World War II.* U.S. Naval Inst. 1953

Sensho Sosho (Boeicho Kenshujo Senshishitsu) [*The Aleutians*] Vol 29. (in Jpnse) Japan Defense Agency. War Hist. Section. Tokyo. n.d.

Watts, Anthony J. and Brian C. Gordon. *The Imperial Japanese Navy.* Doubleday. 1971.

Webber, Bert. *Silent Siege III; Japanese Attacks On North America in World War II, Ships Sunk, Air Raids, Bombs Dropped, Civilians Killed.* Webb Research Group. 1992.

Zacharias, Ellis M. *Secret Missions; the Story of an Intelligence Officer.* Putnam. [1946].

Index

NOTES ABOUT THIS INDEX: Illustration page numbers, names of ships, newspapers, magazines, books are shown in *italic*. As many persons advanced in grade during the war, or received higher grades in later years, we attempt to use the rank held during the incident. Rank is expressed in "base" terms as, all Lieutenants in Army and Navy are expressed as (Lt). The same rule applies to all grades of Admirals, Generals, Sergeants etc. Some jobs, when clarification seems indicated due to similarity in names, are shown in parenthesis as (pilot). The type of military ship is designated in base terms as, all cruisers, light or heavy are shown as (C). Carriers all classes shown as (CV). Battleships (BB). Destroyers and Destroyer-Escorts shown as (DD). Aircraft tenders (AT). Minesweepers (M). Submarines (Sub). Japanese submarines have prefix letters I or RO then a number. Tankers (T). Vessels, if the types are unclear, are shown as *Arcata* (ship). Names of ships, certain other items and individuals, when the name is similar in English and Japanese, the Japanese entry is followed by [J] as: *Tama* [J](C). First names of some persons were not found thus the omissions are acknowledged.

222

223

General M. Okumiya was a career officer for the forces of Japan. He was a graduate of the Imperial Naval Academy at Etajima in 1930 and in 1937 led the air attack that sank the U.S.S. *Panay* in China. Later, as a test pilot proving the potential of the VAL dive-bomber, he crashed and was severely burned. He was grounded due to his severe injuries (his face still bears those scars) but served as Air Officer during the war. He was on the *Junyo*, the 27,500-ton carrier during the Dutch Harbor raids. He was interviewed by Stanton H. Patty for an article, "He Bombed Dutch Harbor," that appeared in the May 1969 issue of the *Alaska Sportsman* and by Bert Webber in Tsuchiura, Japan in 1975 for this book. Okumiya served in both the Navy and Army. General Okumiya's remarks here are based on the two interviews:

If the Battle of Midway had been successful for us, then our attacks on Dutch Harbor also would have been considered successful. As to Attu and Kiska occupation, these were not worthwhile considering the outcome of Midway. To maintain Attu and Kiska, we had to tie up many warships, cargo ships and tankers. That was very expensive. It was never considered seriously that we invade and occupy Alaska itself. If we had such strength we would have invaded Hawaii, not Alaska but our strength was too poor.